THE ART OF IRISH COOKING

THE ART OF IRISH COOKING
by Monica Sheridan

Irish cuisine consists of much more than variations on the potato and **The Art of Irish Cooking** reveals its many aspects. Recipes for traditional favorites like *Corned Beef, Irish Stew* and *Irish Soda Bread* are included, as well as recipes for hearty soups, savory seafood and poultry dishes, nutritious vegetables, and delicious breads and cakes.

Other Cookbooks in Our International Classics Series:

THE CUISINE OF ARMENIA *available in January 1996* 0-7818-417-5 $14.95pb

THE ART OF BRAZILIAN COOKERY *Dolores Botafogo* 0-7818-0130-3 $9.95pb

THE JOY OF CHINESE COOKING *Doreen Yen Hung Feng* 0-7818-0097-8 $8.95pb

ALL ALONG THE DANUBE *Marina Polvay* 0-7818-0098-6 $11.95pb

THE BEST OF FINNISH COOKING *Taimi Previdi* 0-7818-0284-9 $19.95hc

THE ART OF HUNGARIAN COOKING *Paula Pogany Bennett & Velma R. Clark* 0-7818-0202-4 $8.95pb

THE ART OF ISRAELI COOKING *Chef Aldo Nahoum* 0-7818-0096-X $9.95pb

THE ART OF PERSIAN COOKING *Forough Hekmat* 0-87052-123-3 $8.95pb

POLISH HERITAGE COOKERY *Robert and Maria Strybel* 0-7818-0069-2 $35.00 hc

THE BEST OF RUSSIAN COOKING *Alexandra Kropotkin* 0-7818-0131-1 $9.95pb

A SPANISH FAMILY COOKBOOK *Juan and Susan Serrano* 0-7818-0193-1 $9.95pb

THE BEST OF SMORGASBORD COOKING *Gerda Simonson* 0-7818-0407-8 $14.95pb

THE ART OF TURKISH COOKING *Neset Eren* 0-7818-0201-6 $12.95pb

THE BEST OF UKRAINIAN CUISINE *Bohdan Zahny* 0-7818-0240-7 $19.95 hc

The Art of
IRISH COOKING

MONICA SHERIDAN

Illustrated by Reisie Lonette

FOREWORD BY ROBERT BRISCOE
Former Mayor of Dublin

HIPPOCRENE BOOKS
New York

First published in 1965 by Doubleday & Co.
Hippocrene paperback edition 1996.

All rights reserved.

For information, address:
HIPPOCRENE BOOKS, INC.
171 Madison Avenue
New York, NY 10016

Library of Congress Cataloging-in-Publication Data
Sheridan, Monica.
      The art of Irish cooking / Monica Sheridan ; illustrated by
Reisie Lonette ; foreword by Robert Briscoe. -- Hippocrene pbk. ed.
     p. cm.
     Originally published: Garden City, N.Y. : Doubleday, 1965.
     Includes index.
     ISBN 0-7818-0454-X
     1. Cookery, Irish. I. Title.
TX717.5.S52 1996   95-51183
641.59415--dc20   CIP

Printed in the United States of America.

For our daughter
CATHERINE

recalling those words of Yeats:

Cast your mind on other days
That we in coming days may be
Still the indomitable Irishry.

Foreword

I AM proud to introduce this book to the American public, especially to the many millions with Irish connections or with Irish blood in their veins.

Having made many friends among them on my visits to the United States, I know that—even to the third and fourth generation—they cherish a warm, nostalgic (if sometimes inaccurate) image of Ireland somewhere in their hearts. Monica Sheridan's book will revive for them, in more senses than one, the true flavour of their heritage—for she has distilled a wonderfully rich mixture of knowledge, experience, and humour into this practical and stimulating guide to the art of Irish cooking.

Apart from its practical value, THE ART OF IRISH COOKING will come as a shock to any benighted folk who may still think of Ireland as a primitive country where the people subsist mainly on potatoes, porridge, and buttermilk. The many Americans who come to visit us each year are, of course, familiar with the real Ireland: a modern democracy with a fast-growing economy, the world's highest calorie-intake, and a vigorous, healthy population.

An acknowledged expert in her field, Mrs. Sheridan, in her carefully chosen recipes and her vivid and readable comments, shows us the development of Irish cooking as a living art—the product of an age-old culture, and of a society in which the family—and the proper nourishment of the family—has been a primary concern of every generation. The advent of modern equipment and new cooking methods has, of course, brought fresh development and greatly widened the scope and variety of the typical Irish menu in our homes, hotels, and restaurants.

On the domestic scene, the author of this book (through her writing and her television programmes) has made an outstanding contribution. She has inspired countless Irish viewers and readers to experiment by varying and refining on the basic recipes handed down from earlier generations. For her enthusiastic followers the results have opened up new and exciting horizons in the world of food.

It will be seen that Mrs. Sheridan combines sophistication and simplicity in her treatment of those fresh, natural ingredients which have always been the basis of the typical Irish diet. Where food is abundant it is sometimes necessary to tempt the palate, and here is the most skilful temptress since Eve served up that apple.

But even in less plenteous times, our traditional Irish fare proved itself a boundless source of rugged health and stamina. During the past century it built the muscles that helped to push the great railroads across the American continent, and the Irish intellects that have adorned the world's literature. It nourished, too, the sturdy and gifted stock that gave America one of its outstanding Presidents.

Written with gusto and vivacity, Mrs. Sheridan's book will interest and delight every reader with a palate for good food and good writing. I am sure that her lucid and persuasive guidance will prompt many housewives—in these days of standardisation, processing, and deep-freezing—to rediscover the simple joys of cooking in the natural style.

This is not the only book on cooking I have ever read through. Recipes have always intimidated me, being rather like complicated medical prescriptions. And the detailed instructions usually baffle me entirely. But THE ART OF IRISH COOKING is a dish much more to my liking. It has brought back many nostalgic memories and whetted my appetite for delectable dishes which are still to come.

Here, indeed, is a feast of down-to-earth Irish wisdom, garnished with rare kitchen lore, and spiced with that spontaneous and inimitable wit which has made Monica Sheridan an outstanding journalist and a national television personality in her own country.

I wish you all good appetite and can promise you good reading.

ACKNOWLEDGMENTS

In the writing of this book, I owe a special debt to three people: Kevin Danaher of the Irish Folklore Commission, whose book *In Ireland Long Ago* was a constant source of inspiration; my husband, Niall, who struggled with my spelling and syntax, and our friend Coleman White of Sorrento Cottage, Dalkey, who invited me to work in a room with a view that has no equal on God's earth.

For the Irish sayings which preface each chapter I am grateful to countless generations of anonymous ancestors.

Contents

FOREWORD *by Robert Briscoe*   vii

INTRODUCTION   xv

TYPICAL IRISH MENUS   xxiii

APPETIZERS   1

SOUPS   7

FISH AND SHELLFISH   22

MEATS   46

POULTRY AND GAME   75

A WORD ABOUT EGGS   93

VEGETABLES   100

BREAD AND CAKES   119

PUDDINGS AND PIES   142

BEVERAGES   153

INDEX   161

Recipes for items printed in small capital letters may be located by consulting the Index.

INTRODUCTION

Ní geal an gáire ach san áit a mbíonn an biadh.

(Laughter is gayest where the food is best.)

THERE are said to be some twenty-five million people of Irish descent in the United States. I can well believe it, for I've seldom met an American who couldn't boast of the bones of an Irish grandmother somewhere in the family cupboard of skeletons. So, whether you live in New York or San Francisco, in Chicago or Dallas, it's quite on the cards that some part of your heritage sleeps quietly in the shadow of an Irish country church.

Be that as it may, history and the past are very much part of our lives in Ireland. Perhaps that is why, in thinking about the evolution of Irish cooking, my mind goes back to the country kitchen of my great-grandmother—a good starting point from which to trace the development of our native cuisine, from the basic sustenance of post-Famine days to the simple, varied, and sophisticated fare that nourishes us today.

My great-grandmother lived to be over a hundred, though she never admitted to more than ninety-five. I can still see her clearly in the kitchen of her thatched cottage, with the big turf fire burning on the hearth and the bastable oven suspended from a crook in the chimney breast. There it hung over the red embers, its iron lid smothered in glowing sods of turf and the smell of an Irish stew escaping into the warm kitchen. On the hearth was a wide griddle with a cake of soda bread rising in the friendly heat, and in another corner was the oaten cake propped on an iron toaster and crisping in the rays of the fire.

The kitchen had an earthen floor, a half door, and a small, recessed window, where she could sit and embroider or mend, when she had leisure to sit at all. At the side of the kitchen opposite the door was a dresser, where porridge bowls and cups and patterned plates shone in the soft light. Off the kitchen was the pantry, where there were terra-cotta crocks with a navy-blue glaze around the edges. Here the new milk was stored and soured for the Tuesday churning. The old dash churn stood, like a dragoon, in a dim corner, and around it were the paraphernalia of the buttermaking—the scalded pans, the wooden butter pats with the shamrock, the rose, and the thistle designs so expertly carved on their wooden surfaces.

I can remember, as if it were yesterday, the day my great-grandmother moved from the cottage where she had lived all her married life to a more modern abode. When the day of parting came she refused to budge until a bucketful of live embers was carried to her new home and the fire kindled from them. In her old home the fire—banked up every night—had never been quenched for two hundred years, and she was not going to abandon her luck and her feeling for the dead generations behind her.

Her daughter, my grandmother, married a modest draper, who

had a house with a slated roof and a kitchen with a coal range. She had done well for herself, you might say, because she had exchanged the backbreaking life of the small farmer's wife for the comparative opulence of trade.

Grandmother's kitchen was a luxurious affair, with water that came out of a tap and a gluttonous range that devoured tons of coal, but where a dozen pots could boil on top without her having to scorch her face at the open fire. And there was an oven—a real oven with a door that shut in the heat. Luster jugs now lined the dresser, and fine china cups with paintings of cocks and hens on them. The old dash churn was replaced by the revolving barrel churn, but grandmother continued to make her own butter.

Where my great-grandmother had been content with the most modest of fare—porridge, potatoes and butter, a glass of buttermilk and the occasional piece of salty bacon (she had lived through the Famine and learned to be thankful for the simplest food)—grandmother soon graduated to the more luxurious fare of the merchant princeling. I can still remember the delicious smells that came out of that wondrous kitchen—sugared ham browning in front of the fire; hot toast, speared on a fork and held in front of the red coals; strong tea brewing on a corner of the stove and ammonia buns coming out of the hot oven on a frosty day. Ammonia buns—can you imagine it?—crisp as a biscuit, light as a feather. I have never seen them since, and I don't know how to make them now, but to this day the pungent reek of ammonia brings me right back to my grandmother's kitchen with the hot buns coming out of the oven. Talk about Proust and his *madeleine!*

In that kitchen I first became aware of the sensuous magic of cooking. Tipsy cakes and trifle spiked with almonds, plump chickens (their exuberant brown bosoms glistening with melted butter), squat ducks with fat thighs and brittle, crackling skin. Grandmother was not a great cook, but in her comparative affluence she had learned to be extravagant with food—something her mother would never have tolerated.

All her daughters (my mother and aunts) became wonderful cooks. They could preserve and bottle, make cakes and jams, galantines, and confections. Not only did they absorb the traditional cookery of previous generations, but they spread their culinary wings and enlarged their horizons with new refinements.

When my mother married, she continued to churn her own butter, cure her own bacon, bake her own bread, and make the most outlandish hats with feathers purloined from the cock. She sent her daughters to be educated in fashionable convent schools where, she maintained, they couldn't teach you how to boil an egg.

We had our own cattle and sheep and six milch cows to supply the household with milk. Our kitchen was a large room with a stove that looked like the engine of the *Queen Elizabeth*. Flitches of bacon hung from hooks on the ceiling, and plum puddings too. In those days it was the custom to keep a few puddings over from Christmas to the following harvest. A family of crickets lived behind the stove and their chirruping could be heard loudly when the house was still. They used to eat socks, too, if the socks were left near the stove to air at night. But crickets were considered lucky and no one would have thought to disturb them.

Tara, the dog, lay stretched across the fire at night, his coat positively shining in the lamplight. "And why wouldn't it?" mother said bitterly. "And maybe a dozen of my best eggs under his ribs."

It was perfectly true. Tara had a passion for raw eggs, and every time he heard a hen cackling you would see his ears stand up, and off with him in search of the egg. But Tara was the best gun dog in the county and the apple of my father's eye.

Pushkin, the cat, lay between Tara's front paws, and, if it was a cold January, you might see one or two barrels at the side of the fire and the mournful faces of baby lambs peering out over them. Maybe the mother had died in the snow; maybe she had twins and couldn't feed both.

And always, always, there was that wonderful smell of cooking —a ham simmering at the side of the range, with a wisp of hay in the bottom of the pot; a sultana cake in the oven; apple tarts, pungent with cloves, steaming on the kitchen table; a whole salmon cooling in a fish kettle. And, of course, the washing and ironing. I always associate my childhood with great bundles of clothes, fresh from the clothesline or the thorn hedge, and the hiss of a hot iron easing its way over damp linen.

The pattern of our life was leisurely. "The man who made Time made plenty of it," my father would say. Breakfast, which started at 8 A.M. for the smaller children going off to school, always began with oaten porridge and milk straight from the cow and still warm. Some took their porridge lightly salted as it came from the pot, some sprinkled soft brown sugar on it, while the smaller ones made a hole in the center and dropped a spoonful of honey into it.

The porridge was followed by boiled eggs that had been gathered the night before. All the eggs had to be brown, because nobody in our house would touch a white-shelled egg (a senseless family prejudice). A great cake of brown bread stood at either end of the table, and the one with the strongest arm sliced for the eaters. We had our own butter and our own honey, and all this was washed down by enormous draughts of strong, sweet tea. On Thursday night the bread van called. That was the only time we ever saw "shop" bread. It was a great treat to us to see a white pan loaf, and every Friday morning we had real toast made from the baker's bread. On all Sundays and feast days we had bacon and eggs.

But no matter what else we had the day always started with porridge. We all firmly believed that porridge put the roses in

our cheeks and the curls in our hair. Even my brothers, who
were all outrageously spoiled by Mother, ate it to make them
good footballers.

Dinner in an Irish farmhouse is always in the middle of the
day. Men come in hungry from the fields, children from school.
Soup is bubbling on the range. Potatoes, boiled in their jackets,
are bursting through their brown skins—"laughing," as we used
to say. A crackling roast of beef or pork comes out of the oven.
Spring greens have been tossed into the water where a ham was
boiled. Young gooseberries have been imprisoned in a tart.

The long, thin blade of the carving knife is whetted on the
stone step of the threshold. This is the signal that dinner is
ready. . . .

It's a long time now since I left the simple world of my childhood. For more than thirty years I have lived in the cosmopoli-
tan society of the city. I can rustle up a *coq-au-vin* with the best
of them and can tell the difference between beluga and ostrova
when the caviar comes around. But I'm glad I was reared in a
milieu where all our food came straight from the good earth
around us, where chickens and pigs and lambs lived out their
short lives in the freedom of the open fields.

It was a good life, or so it seems to me at this distance of time,
though I doubt if I would fit so snugly into it now. Time tends
to highlight the simple pleasures, like the purr of a reaper in a
field of corn, or a drift of plover swooping over a hedge, or the
smell of burning toffee in a sunny kitchen. Time, too, blurs the
memory of long, gray winters when the trees were bare and the
fields caked with mud, when fingers and noses were blue with
cold. Why, I wonder, are the memorable days of childhood always lit with sunshine?

In this book I hope to offer you some of the traditional cooking lore of Ireland. In many ways ours is a simple diet, but—as all
the world knows—it has nourished a complex and remarkable as-

sortment of poets and playwrights, politicians and pugilists, actors and orators, philosophers and wits.

Why? It may be the brown bread, or the strong tea, or the oaten porridge, or the whiskey. Read on and draw your own conclusions.

TYPICAL IRISH MENUS

BREAKFAST
Weekday Morning

PORRIDGE   BOILED EGG

WHOLE-MEAL BREAD

BUTTER   IRISH HONEY

STRONG IRISH TEA

Sunday Morning

PORRIDGE   BACON AND EGG

POTATO CAKES

IRISH SODA BREAD   STRONG IRISH TEA

Sunday Morning in County Cork

DRISHEENS WITH TANSY BUTTER

WHOLE-MEAL SCONES   STRONG IRISH TEA

LUNCH
Family Lunch (1)

IRISH STEW   YOUNG CARROTS GLAZED WITH BUTTER

STEWED RHUBARB AND BAKED CUSTARD

Family Lunch (2)

BOILED HAM AND CABBAGE   BAKED POTATOES

ROASTED APPLES

Fridays and Fast Days

IRISH POTATO SOUP   BAKED, STUFFED HADDOCK

COLCANNON   LEMON PUDDING

Visitors' Lunch (1)

(We are now showing off.)

PRAWN COCKTAIL   BROILED LAMB CUTLETS

SPINACH

NEW POTATOES TOSSED IN PARSLEY AND BUTTER

STRAWBERRY FLAN

Visitors' Lunch (2)

SMOKED SALMON   FILLET STEAK

MUSHROOMS

FLOUNCY POTATOES   SALAD

RASPBERRIES AND CREAM

SUNDAY DINNER (1:30 P.M.)

*(Sturdy food for all the family.
Afterward father snores behind the Sunday papers.)*

CELERY SOUP   ROAST BEEF

BUTTERED PARSNIPS

ROAST ONIONS   CHAMP

APPLE TART

ST. PATRICK'S DAY DINNER

CLEAR SOUP

ROAST CHICKEN AND BAKED LIMERICK
HAM

CAULIFLOWER AND CHEESE SAUCE

SALAD   RICED POTATOES

IRISH COFFEE PUDDING

EASTER DINNER

CHICKEN AND HAM SOUP   ROAST SPRING LAMB

FRESH GREEN PEAS

POTATOES TOSSED IN BUTTER   SALAD

TIPSY CAKE

CHRISTMAS DAY DINNER

CLEAR SOUP

ROAST TURKEY, BOILED LIMERICK HAM   SPICED BEEF

CELERY, BRUSSELS SPROUTS

CREAMED POTATOES   WINTER SALAD

CURLED CELERY

PLUM PUDDING, BRANDY BUTTER   MINCE PIES

ALMONDS AND RAISINS

DIVERS CHEESES   FRESH FRUITS

(bicarbonate of soda—you'll need this)

EXPENSE ACCOUNT DINNER
(in a restaurant, autumn)

24 GALWAY OYSTERS   ROAST PHEASANT, BREAD SAUCE

FRENCH BEANS

PANCAKES FLAMED IN IRISH MIST   SEVERAL IRISH
COFFEES

(a tranquilizer with the check)

APPETIZERS

Is maith an t-annlann an t-ocras.

(Hunger is the best sauce.)

When I talk about appetizers here, I am really thinking of starters to a luncheon or supper. You know the sort of thing I mean—slivers of smoked salmon, prawn cocktail, liver pâté, caviar. We Irish are nothing wonderful at the cocktail snacks, which have reached such a stage of perfection in America, and I'd be nervous of offering suggestions. But there is nothing to stop you putting the liver pâté on a biscuit and calling it a canapé. The red caviar is really excellent if you can lay your hands on the fresh roe of a pregnant salmon (is there a fishmonger in your family?). We like to think that Dublin Bay prawns are the best in the world and unique to Ireland, though I suspect that this is a bit of Celtic exaggeration.

And then there are herrings. Heavens, I nearly forgot our pickled herrings, and the tangy flavor of marinated kippers.

LIVER PÂTÉ (1)

¾ pound chicken livers	1 teaspoon salt
2 eggs	Pepper
1 egg yolk	½ teaspoon mixed
2 teaspoons butter	powdered cloves and
1¼ cups light cream or	powdered mace
rich milk	1 bay leaf

Drop the raw livers, which have been relieved of their stringy fibers, into the blender. When they are completely emulsified, add all the rest of the ingredients except the bay leaf. Pour the mixture into a well-buttered fireproof dish, add a dried bay leaf, and cover with aluminum foil. Stand the dish in a pan containing about 1 inch of water and bake in a moderate oven (350°) for 1 hour, reducing heat after the first half-hour.

This pâté can be eaten either hot or cold, but I think it is much nicer cold. It is light and very kind to the digestion. Properly cooked, it should be a faint pink color when you cut into it—not unlike the real *foie gras* (which costs an absolute fortune). By the way, watch that the water in the bottom pan does not boil. You must nurture the pâté as you would a baked egg custard. Serve with thin toast. *6–8 servings.*

LIVER PÂTÉ (2)

½ pound pork or chicken	¼ teaspoon salt
livers	Pepper
2 tablespoons milk	½ teaspoon powdered
½ tablespoon Irish	cloves
whiskey	2 blades mace
1 bay leaf	1 cup butter
1 sprig thyme	

Cut liver in inch cubes and trim away the veins. Leave to marinate in the milk and whiskey and all the seasonings for an hour. Gently poach the liver in the marinade for 20 minutes. When cool discard thyme and bay leaf and emulsify the liver and liquid in a liquidizer. Add the butter in lumps. When everything is well mixed, pour into a dish and chill in the refrigerator.

This is quite good for cocktail snacks, but I think it too rich as a starter for a meal. My sister puts pounded anchovies into the mixture. Me, no likey! *8–10 servings.*

COLD CHICKEN LIVERS

1 *pound chicken livers*	½ *tablespoon Irish whiskey*
1 *teaspoon butter*	¾ *teaspoon salt*
1 *bay leaf*	*Pepper*
6 *cloves*	2 *blades mace*

Put the livers into a buttered small pie dish with all the other ingredients. Cover the dish with aluminum foil. Stand it in a pan of water and bake in a moderate oven (350°) for three-quarters hour. Chill before serving with thin toast.

This is far nicer than it sounds. And the livers, except for the top layer, have a rosy-pink hue. *6–8 servings.*

RED CAVIAR

I have no idea how salmon manage their love life in America, but in Ireland they come up the rivers in the early autumn looking for a suitable place to spawn. Alas, some of these pregnant salmon are inadvertently caught in nets before their accouchement, and they are full of the most delicious roes.

The caviar made from salmon roes is known as red caviar (as if you didn't know). The eggs are much bigger than the sturgeon's—they'd be about the size of No. 2 gunshot—and they are an interesting orange color. A ripe roe can weigh about three-quarters pound, maybe more, maybe less, depending on the size of the mother salmon.

  1 to 2 salmon roes
  2 cups boiling water
  1 teaspoon coarse salt

Put the roes into a warm bowl and cover completely with the boiling water. Cover the bowl and allow to stand for 5 minutes. (The idea of the boiling water is to "set" the membrane so that the eggs can be scraped away from it.) After 5 minutes remove the roes and allow them to cool.

Now comes the delicate part of the operation. With the back of a knife scrape the eggs away from the surrounding skin without bursting them. This requires great patience and tenderness. Sprinkle a generous helping of coarse salt over the eggs and you have your red caviar. Chill in the refrigerator. Serve on toast with a squeeze of lemon. Lovely in an omelet, too.

You can't imagine how delicious this is. The little eggs go pop under your teeth. But I warn you, it won't keep, even in the refrigerator, for more than a couple of days. It never lasted for more than a couple of hours with our family.

P.S. If the roes have been put in the deep freeze, the eggs will burst when you try to strip them. Pity. *6 servings approximately.*

PRAWN COCKTAIL

In Ireland prawns (large shrimp) are considered to be a greater delicacy than lobster.

  24 peeled, cooked prawns
  4 shallow stemmed glasses
  6 lettuce leaves, finely shredded

Put a little of the shredded lettuce in the bottom of each stemmed glass. Lay 6 prawns on top and mask with the following sauce.

PRAWN COCKTAIL SAUCE:

2 tablespoons mayonnaise
2 tablespoons tomato
  ketchup
2 tablespoons whipped
  cream

A dash of Worcester sauce
½ teaspoon grated fresh
  horse-radish
Salt and pepper to taste

Mix all together and pour over the prawns. *4 servings.*

CRAB COCKTAIL

½ pound picked crab meat
½ tablespoon mild vinegar
¼ teaspoon mustard
½ tablespoon chopped
  gherkin

1 tablespoon mayonnaise
1 tablespoon tomato ketchup
1 tablespoon heavy cream,
  whipped

Mix all together, reserving a little of the whipped cream as a top dressing. Serve in individual glasses as for PRAWN COCKTAIL (given above). *6 servings.*

PICKLED HERRINGS

6 herrings
Salt and pepper
½ cup vinegar
1 cup beer
1 onion, sliced
1 carrot, sliced

1 bay leaf
1 bunch parsley
6 cloves
1 sprig thyme
6 peppercorns
1 teaspoon salt

Cut the heads off the herrings. Gut the fish and slit all the way down the belly to the tail. Run your thumb along the backbone and ease the flesh away from the bones. The whole cage of bones should come right out. Lightly salt and pepper the flesh and roll up into a curl. Make an aromatic pickle out of the vinegar and all the other ingredients, boil together for a half-hour. Put the curled herrings in a deep pie dish and pour the pickle over them. Cover with a lid or aluminum foil and bake in a moderate oven (350°) for a half-hour. This dish is served cold and should be kept for at least 24 hours before eating. *6 servings.*

KIPPERS

These are herrings that have been lightly salted and then smoked. Sometimes they are sold on the bone and, for that again, they may be filleted. They are very popular as a Friday breakfast dish in Ireland, where everybody likes to start the day well nourished. Since they are so rich in fat, they are always broiled dry (I mean with no butter on them).

MARINATED KIPPERS

One of the nicest ways to eat kippers is raw. If you like smoked salmon, you are bound to like the following dish. It is really the poor man's smoked salmon.

3 *boned kippers*	1 *onion, sliced*
1 *tablespoon vinegar*	1 *bay leaf*
2 *tablespoons olive oil*	*Black pepper*

Skin the kippers by running a sharp knife between the skin and the flesh. Slice the flesh into strips about the thickness of an anchovy. Leave to marinate in the oil, vinegar, and other flavorings for 24 hours. Drain and eat as an appetizer. It works up a powerful thirst. Very good as an addition to hors d'oeuvres.

SOUPS

B'fhearr an sugh go mór ná an fheoil.

(Soup is the essence of meat.)

THE geography we learn at school tells us that Ireland has a moderate climate, warmed by the Gulf Stream, without any great variations of temperature either in summer or winter. This is a flagrant piece of Celtic exaggeration. We have a mild summer all right, far too mild for comfort, but we *can* get perishing cold winters, especially when the east wind sweeps across from Siberia and gives out its last gasps as it crosses the plains of Ireland. When the east wind isn't blowing, we may be assailed by a deep depression from the west (that would be America), when rain-laden winds blow in from the Atlantic and damp the very marrow in your bones. There are the magic days, too, when the very air is translucent, when all the fields and hedgerows are Kelly green, when ripe corn waves like liquid gold—but we haven't half enough of them.

You wouldn't be long in Ireland before realizing that soup is an essential part of our daily fare. Like whiskey, it is our internal central heating, raising the temperature of the body and thawing out the gastric juices so that they will be receptive to the delights that are to follow. Remember, in Ireland, except in the cities, domestic central heating is still a rarity (we are a credulous people and believe what we read in the geography books). We need soup to warm us. Americans need iced water to cool them off. How ill-balanced the world really is, when you come to think of it.

Of all the things you cook in your kitchen, surely soup is the most personal. It needn't have a name, it need never taste the same, and you may never even remember how you made it. Some of the best family soups are made by tossing together the remains of last night's stew and today's tomato sauce with a few herbs and vegetables. Simmer the lot on the side of the stove, sieve them, add a dollop of cream and you have a wonderful soup for tonight.

The basic principle of all orthodox soup-making (never mind what I've said about the slung-together soup) is to sweat the vegetables in butter before adding any liquid. This brings out the lurking sugar and all those essential oils that distinguish one flavor from another. Naturally, you don't let the diced vegetables get crisped or brown. Only melt them, if you know what I mean. Then in goes the stock or the water and the meat and whatever else you fancy. Clear soup, like the irregular verbs, is the exception that proves the rule, but, since it is the quintessence of all liquid refreshment (barring alcohol), we must forgive it for stepping out of line. More about it later.

*   *   *

The potato is to Ireland what pasta is to the Italians, or rice to the Chinese. Indeed, it was the potato that sustained the Irish through the worst years of oppression, and it was the failure of the potato crop that brought about the Black Famine of the last century. Potatoes keep on cropping up in Irish cooking, as an independent vegetable, as the chassis of an Irish stew, in a variety of native breads. You will find a cut potato left in a jar of tobacco to keep it moist, and you may meet a man on the road who carries a wizened potato in his hip pocket as an antidote for rheumatism.

Think of the lyrical names we give our potatoes . . . Golden Wonders, Aran Banners, Irish Queens, Ulster Chieftains, Dunbar Rovers, Skerry Champions. They read more like crack regiments than modest tubers.

IRISH POTATO SOUP

2 tablespoons butter	Salt and pepper
2 medium onions	1 sprig thyme, 1 bay leaf,
3 large potatoes, peeled	1 bunch parsley, tied
5 cups milk	together
1 clove garlic, crushed	½ cup evaporated milk
2 blades mace	Chopped chives to garnish

Melt the butter in a heavy pan. Add the thinly sliced onions and potatoes. Toss well in the butter. Lay a piece of wax paper or aluminum foil down over the vegetables, as if to tuck them in. This will keep them from drying out. Cover the pan with a lid and allow the vegetables to soften over a slow heat for about 10 minutes. On no account must you let them brown or you will destroy the bland flavor. Now remove the paper (or foil) and add the milk and all the other ingredients except the evaporated milk and chives, which are only for final decoration. Simmer for a half-hour. Discard the thyme, bay leaf, and parsley and sieve the soup. Reheat in a clean saucepan. In the bottom of each soup cup put a tablespoon of evaporated milk and a good scatter of chopped chives. Pour the hot soup on top and give it one stir. Very nice.   6 *servings*.

This soup is even more interesting if you use the stock obtained from boiling chicken bones and a handful of vegetables together for a couple of hours. Let me tell you about it now in case I forget later on.

CHICKEN-BONE STOCK

You have had a chicken, maybe two chickens, for dinner, depending on the size of your family or the depth of your purse. There is nothing now left but the carcass and those spindly leg and thigh bones. Wash the lot in warm water. Now break up the carcass with your hands, so that it will fit in the saucepan, add the legs, which you have cut through with a poultry shears or crushed with a hammer (there is all that lovely chicken marrow inside). Throw in an onion cut in half and a carrot ditto and don't neglect a half-dozen cloves and peppercorns and a shake of salt, and cover all with four cups of cold water. (The cloves make a wonderful smell in the kitchen.) Let this simmer in the oven or on the stove for a couple of hours. Strain off through a fine sieve, being careful to capture all splinters, and hold the chicken liquid in a jug in the refrigerator until the next time you are making soup.

By the way, turkey bones are even better. And as for the carcasses of game and ducks—lovely!

PALE ONION SOUP

After potatoes, onions are the most important vegetable in an Irishwoman's kitchen. They give that certain zest to an Irish stew, they enliven all soups, and they make you cry when you peel them. Caitlin ni Houlihan and Deirdre of the Sorrows both got their doleful countenances from the fierce, pungent oil that escapes from the particular breed of onion we grow in Ireland. In the early spring the onion ridges are thinned out and the slim green shoots are known as scallions. These are eaten raw or are finely chopped and added to mashed potatoes. The fat, matronly onions are turned into soup.

If you dip an onion in cold water before skinning it, this will make you less tearful.

ONION SOUP

4 large onions	½ teaspoon powdered
1½ tablespoons butter	mace
1½ tablespoons flour	Salt and pepper
2 cups boiling milk	2 egg yolks
1 bay leaf	½ cup evaporated milk
2 cups CHICKEN-BONE STOCK	or cream
(given above)	

Melt the thinly sliced onions in the butter until translucent. Shake the flour into the onions and stir well to absorb the butter. Gradually add the boiling milk, in which you have infused the bay leaf. Careful that the soup doesn't lump! Now add the chicken stock and seasonings. Simmer until the onions are cooked.

Beat the egg yolks and evaporated milk (or cream) together.

Put them in the bottom of a tureen and gradually add the hot soup as you stir.

If you don't want to bother with a tureen put a little of the yolk-cream mixture in the bottom of each soup bowl, ladle the hot soup on top, and give it a stir or two. Can you follow this? *8 servings.*

CELERY SOUP

Never make celery soup with the white hearts of celery. It is much more sensible to eat them raw. The outer stalks, some of the leaves, and the well-scrubbed root make an excellent soup.

2 *heads celery (minus the good hearts)*	1 *bay leaf*
	4 *cups* CHICKEN-BONE STOCK
2 *peeled potatoes (for thickening)*	*Pepper and salt*
	1 *cup evaporated milk or cream*
2 *medium onions*	½ *nutmeg, grated*
1½ *tablespoons butter*	
2 *cloves garlic, crushed*	

Chop the celery stalks and a few of the top leaves. Slice the potatoes and onions and sweat all three vegetables in the butter until they are soft. Add the crushed garlic, bay leaf, stock, and seasoning. Simmer for a half-hour. Discard the bay leaf. Sieve, reheat, and pour into soup cups to which you have added 1 tablespoon (each) of evaporated milk, or cream, and some grated nutmeg.

p.s. This soup is sometimes made of half milk and half stock. If you use milk, you would be wise to omit the top leaves of the celery, as these are inclined to cause curdling. I use the potatoes as a thickener because it is so much easier than having to use another saucepan to make a binding sauce (one must think of the washing up). *6–8 servings.*

I find that evaporated milk is splendid for all bland soups—far smoother than cream, and easier on the liver, I would say.

ARTICHOKE SOUP

I was a grown woman before I first tasted artichokes. I am, of course, talking about Jerusalem artichokes, those irregular tubers that look like potatoes with warts on them. They are not to be confused with the delicious globe artichokes, with the pull-off leaves, that are so beloved of salivating French gourmets.

Artichoke is perhaps the most delicate of all the vegetable soups. It is made in exactly the same way as celery soup, except that you substitute peeled artichokes for the celery. It has the great advantage that Jerusalem artichokes are very cheap. They are the Cinderellas of the vegetable world. It is rather snob to put a few crushed, roasted hazelnuts on top before serving.

LEEK SOUP

The very same as ONION SOUP, except that you substitute 12 "swans' necks" (i.e., the white part of the leeks) for the onions. This is a very gentle soup.

PEA SOUP

Peas played an important part in the diet of the ancient Irish. At one time they even made bread of crushed dried peas. It may have been wholesome, but I'd say it wouldn't have been too easy on the eye.

1 cup dried peas	1 sprig mint
½ teaspoon baking soda	1 sprig thyme
2 medium onions	1 leaf of sage or pinch of
1 large potato	dried sage
1 tablespoon butter or	1 bay leaf
bacon drippings	Salt and pepper
4 cups water or stock	1 teaspoon green vegetable
1 bunch parsley	dye

Soak the peas overnight in 2 cups of boiling water and the soda. Next day wash them to remove the soda.

Melt the sliced onions and potatoes in the fat. Add peas and all other ingredients except the green dye. Boil gently until peas are soft. Remove herbs with a slotted spoon. Add the green dye. Sieve, and serve with cubes of bread that have been fried in bacon fat. *6–8 servings.*

NETTLE TONIC

I don't know whether nettles grow in America, but there is certainly no shortage of them in Ireland, where city dwellers look upon them as noxious weeds. How dare they! Although they have a vicious sting in their leaves, young nettles are full of iron and all classes of fancy vitamins. When cooked they taste rather like spinach, only more delicate. They are included in the diet of race horses and greyhounds, and if you lived in Ireland you would soon realize that what was considered good enough for our four-footed heroes was more than adequate for mere human beings.

1 *pound young nettles*
Boiling water
½ *teaspoon salt*

Wash the nettles well in several waters, wearing protective gloves. Put them into a saucepan and cover with boiling salted water. Cook very gently on top of the stove for a half-hour. Strain and drink a tumblerful, hot or cold, first thing in the morning. Guaranteed to put roses in your cheeks and a glint in your eye. Not pleasant, of course, but you must suffer to be beautiful.

MUTTON BROTH

1 2-*pound neck of mutton*
8 *cups cold water*
2 *tablespoons pearl barley*
2 *teaspoons salt*
Pepper
1 *cup chopped carrots*
1 *white turnip, chopped*

1 *cup chopped leeks*
1 *cup chopped onions*
1 *cup chopped celery*
2 *cloves garlic, cut up*
½ *cup chopped parsley*
Extra chopped parsley for garnish

Cut the mutton into 7 or 8 pieces. Put into a pan with the water and bring slowly to a boil. Remove the scum that will have risen to the top. Add the barley, salt and pepper and simmer gently for 1½ hours. Add all the vegetables and simmer for another hour until the vegetables are soft and melting but still keeping their shape. Remove the meat from the bone, chop very finely, and add to soup. Garnish with chopped parsley. This is a standard winter soup in Ireland. *8–10 servings.*

CHICKEN AND HAM SOUP

Since boiled chicken is traditionally served in Ireland with a piece of boiled ham or bacon to "stretch" it, it is usual to add a cup or two of the ham water to the water in which the chicken has been boiled. This gives a distinctive flavor.

The soup is followed by the fowl, smothered in PARSLEY SAUCE (given below).

2 tablespoons barley	1 sprig thyme
3 cups water	1 bay leaf
3 cups CHICKEN-BONE STOCK	A pinch of powdered cloves
2 to 3 cups ham water	A pinch of powdered mace
(depending on how	Pepper
salty it is)	1 cup chopped carrots
1 large chicken	1 cup chopped onions
1 bunch parsley	Chopped parsley to garnish

Steep the barley in 3 cups of water for 2 hours before using. Boil the three liquids—strained barley water, stock, and ham water. Add the chicken, herbs, spices, and barley. Poach for a half-hour. Add the chopped vegetables and continue to simmer until the chicken is tender. This generally takes 1 hour, but you will know when the leg feels soft and springy under the pressure of your finger. Turn off the heat. Let the bird "set" for 10 minutes in the liquid. Put the bird on a warm dish, cover generously with parsley sauce, and serve as the main course.

Taste the soup for seasoning. Discard the parsley, thyme, and bay leaf and serve with a good sprinkling of freshly chopped parsley.

By the way, if you have no ham water, a ham-bone added to the pot is just as good. Improves the flavor of the chicken, too. 8–10 servings.

PARSLEY SAUCE:

1 bunch parsley	1 pinch powdered mace
1½ cups milk	3 tablespoons butter
1½ cups strained CHICKEN	3 tablespoons flour
AND HAM SOUP (given	Salt and pepper
above)	

Scald the parsley in the milk and soup with the pinch of mace. Melt the butter, add the flour, and cook for 1 minute. Strain the boiling liquid, add gradually to the flour and butter mixture to make a smooth sauce. Cook for 10 minutes. Chop the scalded parsley very finely and add to the sauce. Season.

This is a traditional sauce that is slightly green in color. The parsley is a bright emerald.

KIDNEY SOUP

½ beef kidney	1 cup chopped potatoes
1 pound shin beef	1 teaspoon sugar
1 good tablespoon bacon	8 cups water
drippings	1 bay leaf
1 cup chopped carrots	1 bunch parsley
1 cup chopped onions	1 sprig thyme
1 cup chopped white	6 peppercorns
turnips	Salt

Toss sliced kidney and chopped meat in drippings. Add vegetables and sugar. Toss again and allow to color slightly. Add liquid and other ingredients. Simmer for 2 hours and sieve. A can of tomatoes is good added to this soup, but this is a modern refinement. *8–10 servings.*

CLEAR SOUP

This is a distillation made of meat, perfumed with vegetables and sweet-smelling herbs. It is as clear as whiskey, as stimulating as champagne (well, nearly), and as nourishing as stout. It is traditionally served in Ireland as a start to the Christmas dinner.

2½ pounds shin beef	1 bay leaf
12 cups cold water	1 bunch parsley
2 large onions	1 sprig thyme
2 carrots	1 veal bone or 1 pig's foot
2 stalks celery	Salt
1 leek	2 egg whites
8 cloves	1 jigger Irish whiskey
10 peppercorns	

Cut the meat into cubes. Put into cold water together with all the other ingredients except the egg whites and the Irish whiskey. The onions should be cut in two across the waistline, but they should not be skinned. The carrots are scrubbed but not scraped. They are used whole. The celery is simply washed, and likewise the leek. The idea of keeping the vegetables uncut is to prevent them from falling apart and clouding the soup. All you want is their flavor; when the soup is finished you throw them out.

Let the soup simmer at the side of the fire for 5 or 6 hours. Skim it if it forms a scum. Strain through a muslin cloth that has been wrung out in cold water and placed over a sieve.

The next job is to clear it. Put the strained soup in a clean saucepan. Add the 2 egg whites and whisk the whole thing rapidly, while the soup comes slowly to a boil. Then stop whisking and let the liquid simmer for a half-hour, taking care not to break the crust. Wring a clean cloth out in water, place over a strainer, and pour the soup through it, holding back the crust with a spoon. Return the liquid to the heat, add the Irish whiskey, and correct the seasoning. Sure, it's a lot of trouble!

A good consommé should not be brown, as you often see it in a restaurant. A light amber is the correct color, so clear that you should be able to read small print at the bottom of the soup plates. *8 servings.*

TURTLE SOUP

I have never made turtle soup, but, since it is the classic among all soups, I pass on the following information that I got from a Mr. Mooney, who was a celebrated chef in Dublin at the turn of the century.

In those days live turtles were shipped to Dublin from Liverpool, (the best turtles still come from the East Indies and parts of South America to the port of Liverpool).

It was a common sight to see six or eight turtles crawling around the floor of the caterer's shop, each bearing the name of the future host on its back—the Lord Lieutenant, the Lord Mayor, Kings Inns, the Duke of Leinster, the Archbishop.

The turtles were killed by tying a rope around the neck, to prevent the head from being drawn back into the shell. Another rope was tied around the fins and the animal was strung up to a hook in the ceiling. The head was then sawed off and the turtle was left to bleed for two days. The head was put aside in the larder and, for days afterward, it could be seen to nod in a lifelike fashion on the plate.

When the turtle was drained of blood, the meat was filleted away from the shell, cut into lumps, and cooked for nine or ten hours in CLEAR SOUP, mentioned in the previous recipe. Part of the flesh of a turtle resembles veal, part of it is like chicken, and some of it could be taken for fish. The fins are looked upon, by many English gourmets, as the most delicious of entrées.

Madeira is the traditional lacer for turtle soup, but, according to Mr. Mooney, there is nothing that brings out the flavor like a little rum.

It's interesting in a gruesome way, don't you think? But, honestly, can you *see* yourself making turtle soup?

SHELLFISH SOUP

There is a traditional French recipe for *bisque d'homard* in which a fresh lobster, a few vegetables, a half bottle of white wine, a shot of cream, and a good jorum of brandy are all slung together, to emerge as a rich (and very expensive) soup.

I doubt if anybody in this workaday world would throw a glass of brandy into the soup pot and then set a match to it. Certainly I couldn't bring myself to do it, and I know where my husband would put the brandy.

It is an interesting (and shocking) thought that if you boil a lobster it can lose over a quarter of its original weight by the time it is cooked. What becomes of this mysterious quarter? It cannot even be discounted as shell because that comes out of the pot as it went in. I'm afraid the lost quarter represents the very quintessence of the flavor, which has been sucked out into the water. That should give you food for thought the next time you throw away the water in which you have boiled lobsters, prawns, or crabs.

1 *large potato*	1 *bunch parsley*
1 *onion*	1 *pinch saffron*
1 *tablespoon butter*	1 *bay leaf*
2 *cloves garlic*	6 *cups fish stock*
2 *pints any shellfish*	1 *bunch edible seaweed to*
(*mussels, cockles, clams,*	*strengthen the sea taste*
frozen fish, or all	Cream
assorted)	Additional parsley, chopped

Melt the chopped potato and onion in butter. Add shellfish and other ingredients. Bring to boil. Remove fish from shells. Strain soup. Add shelled fish. Serve topped with cream and chopped parsley. *6–8 servings.*

SMOKED FISH SOUP

Perhaps the most distinctive of all family soups is a simple concoction made by boiling together:

2 *onions*	1 *bay leaf*
2 *carrots*	2 *cloves garlic*
1 *large potato*	6 *cups water or fish stock*
2 *tablespoons butter*	1 *sprig thyme*
1 *smoked haddock, 1½ to*	*Cream*
2 pounds	½ *nutmeg, grated*
1 *bunch parsley*	

Melt chopped onions, carrots, and peeled potato in butter. Add fish and other ingredients except the cream and the nutmeg. Simmer till vegetables and fish are cooked. Remove bones from fish and return flesh to soup. Discard parsley and thyme and bay leaf. Sieve soup. Reheat. Serve topped with cream and grated nutmeg. This is very good. *6–8 servings.*

FISH AND SHELLFISH

Sláinte an bhradáin chugat.

(May you be as healthy as the salmon.)

IN THE following section I have, perhaps, overemphasized shellfish, without giving a fair share of space to some of the white fish. There is a personal reason for this. We live beside the sea, so we can buy crabs, lobsters, mussels, prawns, scallops, etc., quite cheaply from the fishermen at the harbor.

We carry them home alive in a bucket and sometimes we bring a can of sea water along. Even if we don't cook the fish in it, the sea water is wonderful for boiling potatoes in. (These are potatoes that are scrubbed but not peeled.) Whatever alchemy is in sea water, the skins of the potatoes never burst. They come out like balls of flour.

When I talk about fish in this section I mean fresh fish, as distinct from frozen fish. The domestic deep-freeze is a rarity in Ireland, and it is my personal opinion that fish is not improved by freezing. I remember once cooking a frozen salmon, and I was shocked by the complete change of both flavor and texture —certainly it was not for the better.

I did discover a very interesting thing about cooking sea fish —salmon, cod, hake, haddock, etc. It should be poached in very salty water. My mother would put three or four fistfuls of kitchen salt into the pot when she was poaching a salmon. The fish did not take up the taste of the salt, but the flesh remained very moist and delicate when it was cooked. I have since found (by trial and error) that the same thing holds true of cod, hake, haddock. The flesh seems to have an infinite tolerance for salt, and it *does* keep in the flavor. This is really quite logical, since the fish are conditioned to the strong brine of the sea, and, even if you broil them, there is no suspicion of salt in the flesh. Mind you, this trick applies to a cut of the fish as well as to the whole fish, but I would be very chary about trying it with fish that had come out of a deep-freeze.

King Salmon

Surely salmon must be the king of all fish; it even looks majestic, as it lies on a slab, its whole body shining like silver sequins.

From the earliest times it was prized as a great delicacy and took pride of place at the banquets of the kings of Ireland. In those days it was boiled in a huge caldron or put on a spit and roasted, while the cook rubbed salt and honey into the flesh. Cormac Mac Art, an early high king of Ireland (we had several lesser kings), was choked by the bone of a salmon that stuck in his throat. He died, poor man.

Salmon is at its very best in the early spring, when it comes in from the ocean and makes its way back up the river where it was born. When the fish come in from the sea they are plump and carefree. In their bodies they have stored up plenty of fat— because it is only in the salt sea that salmon feed. When they come into the rivers they live on their surplus avoirdupois. A salmon fresh from the sea still has the sea lice on it. That is why, if you live beside a salmon river, you will see the salmon leaping out of the water. The sea lice are tickling him and he is trying to shake them off. He is not after flies at all, as many people think.

THE WHOLE SALMON

Slit the salmon along the belly and remove the gut. Scrape away the congealed blood that lies beside the backbone. Remove the gills, as these can give a bitter taste, but keep the head on. Rub the whole salmon over with soft butter. Wrap it well in wax paper or aluminum foil, as if it were a parcel. Put the parcel in a large roasting pan. Bake in a moderate oven (350°), allow-ing 10 minutes to the pound. Let the salmon cool slightly be-fore removing it from the paper. This will give the flesh a chance to set. Carefully skin the fish. Put it on a long plate and garnish it with cucumber. If you want to eat the fish cold, do not un-wrap it for a couple of hours.

This is an interesting way to cook salmon, because the flesh remains an orangey pink (salmon pink) and tastes subtly dif-ferent from that of poached salmon. It has the added advantage that you can cook the whole fish without all that nonsense of a fish kettle. Naturally, you could cook a piece of salmon in the same way but with less time in the oven. A 5-pound salmon should serve 8 to 10 people.

MAYO POACHER'S SALMON

The nicest salmon I have ever eaten was "poached" by a County Mayo man out of an adjacent salmon river at dead of night. He wrapped the fish (it must have weighed 15 pounds) in a thick coating of mud and put it on the hearth to cook in the turf embers. When the mud was hard he cracked it with a hammer. What a perfect salmon was revealed!

POACHED SALMON

> *2-pound cut of fresh salmon*
> *Enough water to cover*
> *½ cup salt*

Bring the water and salt to the boil. Put in the piece of salmon. Cook with the lid off at a gentle simmer for 10 minutes. Remove the saucepan from the heat. Put the lid on the saucepan and let the fish finish cooking in the warm liquid. When the water has come down to about the temperature of a hot bath (test with your finger), lift out the fish. Now skin and serve with melted butter or with any sauce you fancy. *4 servings.*

It is important that salmon should be served *warm*, rather than hot from the boiling pot. There is nothing that dries out quicker than steaming fish. Doesn't taste half as good, either.

COLD SALMON

Prepare it in the same manner as for poached salmon, but leave the fish to get quite cold in the water. It is better to hold cold salmon in a cool larder if you have one. Otherwise take the cooked fish out of the refrigerator and let it stand in the warmth of the kitchen for at least a half-hour before you serve it. To eat salmon that is refrigerator-cold is an injustice to such a majestic fish. As a matter of fact, it is an injustice to any fish.

BROILED SALMON STEAKS

2 *salmon steaks, each* 1¼ *inches thick*	*Sprinkle of salt*
Butter	*Parsley butter* (*given below*)

Butter the steaks generously on both sides. Put under (or over) a hot broiler. Turn after 3 minutes and cook a further 3 minutes. Salt, garnish with parsley butter—a knob of soft butter, a teaspoon of chopped parsley, a good squeeze of lemon, all mixed together. Water cress looks nice with broiled salmon. *2 servings*.

P.S. Never salt anything *before* broiling, for the salt draws out the juice (this is particularly true of steak). Salt just before serving, then you can taste the salt.

STEAMED SALMON

2 *salmon steaks, each* 1¼ *inches thick*	*A squeeze of lemon*
Butter	*A pinch of salt*
	Pepper

Butter an ovenproof plate generously. Lay the steaks on the buttered plate, add a squeeze of lemon. Cover with a lid and put the plate resting over a saucepan of boiling water. Turn the steaks after 4 minutes and allow another 4 minutes for the other side. (Time depends on the thickness of steaks, but they should not be too thick or they will be difficult to cook through.) Add salt and pepper and serve with their own cooking juice. This is really superb. *2 servings*.

FISHERMAN'S SMOKED SALMON

Before the invention of matches the fishermen in the West of Ireland always brought a few sods of lighted turf (in a three-legged pot) in the boats with them when they went out fishing for salmon. These smoldering sods provided a means of lighting their pipes.

When the fishermen set off in the morning, they rarely returned until nightfall. The smoldering embers in the bottom of the pot did not give out sufficient heat on which to cook a proper dinner, but the men did manage to produce a rather recherché smoked salmon.

This is what they did. The salmon was gutted and boned. The two sides were opened out and the fish speared on two thin rods. The rods rested on the lip of the pot, while the salmon hung over the cool smoke. It was left this way for hours. Eaten straight off the pot, it was delicious, but, left to get quite cold, it was without peer.

Cut across the grain, as is the modern smoked salmon, it gave an extraordinarily pleasing effect. The white curd—to be found only in absolutely fresh salmon—alternated with the pink grain of the fish, giving a curiously marbled effect.

This particular smoked salmon later enjoyed quite a vogue with epicures. It has disappeared with the invention of cheap matches and is quite unknown, even among fishermen, any more.

Cod, Hake, Haddock

These can all be cooked in exactly the same way as the salmon. They have much less fat in their bodies, so you will have to be more generous with the butter and cook them for a shorter time.

Did you know that haddock has a special brown mark on its flank? This is supposed to be the thumbprint of St. Peter, left when he hauled the fish into the boat. I can't imagine what haddock were doing over in the Sea of Galilee. Surely they would die with the heat. The Johnny Dory also has the thumbprint. The French call it the St. Pierre. It is a remarkably ugly fish that is found only in our northern waters. The flesh is more delicate than that of sole. Ah well, you can't expect all the fish to look like piscine film stars.

STUFFED FILLETS OF HADDOCK
(OR ANY OTHER WHITE FISH)

2 1-pound fillets of
  haddock
1 cup white breadcrumbs
2 cloves garlic, crushed
1 tablespoon chopped
  parsley
½ teaspoon chopped thyme
1 tablespoon melted butter
Salt and pepper
½ cup cream
2 cups mashed potatoes
1 egg (separated)

Lay a fillet of haddock in a buttered casserole. Make a savory stuffing from the breadcrumbs, garlic, parsley, thyme, melted butter, and seasonings. Put this on top of the fish and cover with the second fillet. Moisten with the cream. Cover and bake in a moderate oven (350°) for 15 minutes. Now take out of the oven and cover with the mashed potatoes, to which the yolk and the stiffly beaten white of the egg have been added. Return to the oven and brown. *4 servings.*

CREAMED SMOKED HADDOCK
(OR ANY OTHER SMOKED WHITE FISH)

2 pounds smoked haddock
⅓ cup olive oil
⅓ cup evaporated milk
2 cloves garlic
Pepper

Poach the haddock in water for 10 minutes. Drain fish. Remove and discard bones and skin. Put fish into the blender with all the other ingredients and blend until it looks like mashed potatoes. Add more evaporated milk if the mixture is too thick. Reheat the mixture in a clean saucepan. Stir with a wooden spoon to prevent sticking. Do not boil. Serve with rice that has been boiled with a pinch of saffron to bring up a yellow contrast to the white creamed fish.

This is a surprisingly pleasant dish. *4 servings.*

CREAMED SALT COD

Substitute salt cod for the smoked haddock in the previous recipe. Soak the salt cod overnight in cold water to soften, and continue as for CREAMED SMOKED HADDOCK. This dish is equally good except that you do not have the smoky flavor of the haddock.

COD'S ROE

I have a feeling that all roes must be very good for you. Think of the thousands of fish they would produce if they only got the chance. Fried cod's roe is a great breakfast dish in Ireland.

1 raw cod's roe of 1 to 1½ pounds
Warm water
Salt

When you buy a raw cod's roe, you must get the whole roe without the membrane having been broken. Wrap the roe in a square of fine cheesecloth. Drop it into warm, salted water. Bring the water to a bubble very slowly. Poach the roe for a half-hour with the lid off the pan, so that you can keep an eye on the movement of the liquid. Fast-boiling water may burst the membrane. When cooked, remove from water and allow to cool completely. Next day, slice down in rings about a half-inch thick. Toss in seasoned flour and fry in butter. Serve with wedges of lemon. This has a nice gritty texture to the teeth. *4–6 servings.*

Trout, Sole

CURED TROUT

I am simply mad about smoked salmon. All my life I have wondered how it was smoked or what strange unguents were rubbed into it before it was hung on a rail in the smokehouse. I don't even know now. But I *can* cure a trout, and it is very nice indeed, I promise you.

1 4-pound pink-fleshed trout	⅓ cup of good olive oil
1½ tablespoons salt	1 tablespoon brown sugar

Cut the trout down the belly and take out the gut. Cut off the head and, with a sharp knife, fillet the flesh away from the bones and whip out the backbone. (Can you follow all this?) When this operation is over, you have the whole, boneless fish, lying on the kitchen table. The skin is, of course, still on the fish, and it stays there. If you are squeamish about boning a trout, the fishmonger will do it for you. It is quite simple, really.

Now put the fish on a platter with the fleshy side up. Rub it all over with a half tablespoon of salt, and leave it for 24 hours in a cool larder or in the warmest part of your refrigerator. (There's a puzzle for you!)

On the second day, mop up any moisture from the melted salt and rub the fish over with good olive oil, massaging it well into the flesh with your fingers.

Third day — same as the first day, a half tablespoon of salt.
Fourth day — same as the second day, oil.
Fifth day — same as the first day, a half tablespoon of salt.
Sixth day — oil and brown sugar.
Seventh day — hang in a current of air to firm.
Eighth day — sliver it off like smoked salmon and eat it with a good squeeze of lemon.

I know all this sounds incredibly tedious (it took only six days to make the world), but it is not really troublesome if you except the boning of the fish. Serves a dozen or more if you are a clever carver.

BROILED BLACK SOLE

In Ireland it is customary to cook sole on the bone. It is a game fish and all the better for being about 36 hours out of the water. Because of its popularity on the menus of our fashionable restaurants, sole is always expensive. When I cook it for my husband, I go to great pains to impress upon him that it made heavy inroads on the housekeeping account. I wouldn't dream of spending that much on a mere guest.

1 sole
Melted butter

Make an incision about 1½ inches long halfway down the spine of the fish. Make 2 pockets on either side of the incision with a sharp knife and insert a piece of butter into each of these. This will keep the flesh from becoming dried up. Now brush the fish with melted butter and put it under the broiler, resting on a piece of greased aluminum foil, until the uppermost side looks cooked—about 2 to 3 minutes, according to size. Turn and cook on the other side. The foil will keep the fish from sticking. *1 serving.*

All the more exotic methods of treating sole you will find in any reliable cookery book.

Flounders, brill, and halibut, which all belong to the flatfish family, are mostly filleted. In home cooking they are simply tossed in flour and fried in butter. In restaurants they do all sorts of fancy things with them, but that is another story altogether.

Whiting

There is a superabundance of whiting in Ireland, but, like everything that is plentiful and cheap, it is looked down upon by the epicures.

WHITING FILLETS

Here is a simple way to cook small fillets of whiting (or any other white fish) for children. I don't recommend it for dyspeptic adults who have to worry about their ulcers or their livers or their waistlines.

4 tablespoons flour	*¼ cup cold water*
½ teaspoon baking powder	*4 small fillets whiting*
Salt and pepper	*Hot oil for frying*
A pinch of herbs	

Mix the flour, baking powder, seasonings, and herbs with the water (no lumps, please) until you have a batter that is about the consistency of thick cream. Put the fillets into this and when they are well coated drop them, one at a time, into a pan of smoking-hot oil. The batter will puff up and become very crisp, while the fish is moist and succulent inside. *2 servings.*

The baking powder is the trick employed by fish-and-chip shops and was kept as a trade secret for generations. By the way, you do *not* use a fish basket, because the batter will stick to it.

Herrings

Herrings have always played an important part in the diet of the Irish. They have so much to recommend them. They are cheap, they are full of nourishment and vitamins. Unfortunately, they are also full of bones. Unless you are clever at easing the flesh from the spine, you could get the impression that you were eating a pincushion. All along our western seaboard it has been the custom of the fishermen to lay down barrels of salted herrings against the winter days when the weather is too stormy to put to sea.

Herrings, like mackerel, are perishable fish and should by rights be eaten within sight of the sea.

FRIED HERRINGS

2 herrings
2 tablespoons Irish
    oatmeal

Butter for frying
Coarse salt

Roll the fresh herrings in the oatmeal. Fry in a thick pan that has been greased with butter. Drain on absorbent paper and season with coarse salt. Traditionally, herrings are eaten with potatoes that have been boiled in their jackets in a pot of sea water. Serve with lemon wedges. *1 or 2 servings.*

BROILED HERRINGS

2 *herrings*
A *little dry mustard*
Salt

Rub the fish with the mustard and broil over a clear fire. Season with salt. This is nicest of all when done in the open air. *1 or 2 servings.*

HERRING ROES

There are two distinct types of roe. There is the gritty roe that comes from the female herring and is made up of thousands of little eggs. And there is the soft, milky roe that is the melt of the male herring. Both are delicious—if you like roes.

1 *pound herring roes*   *Butter for frying*
A *pinch of salt*   *Lemon juice*
½ *cup flour*   *Black pepper*

Toss the roes in the salted flour. Fry gently in butter in a heavy pan. Sprinkle with lemon juice and black pepper. Serve on rounds of buttered toast. *6 servings.*

Mackerel

Like herring, mackerel is very rich in oil, but it is a lot less prolific in bones. If mackerel were as expensive as trout, it would be considered one of the top-ranking fish. But it is a very poor traveler. A few hours out of the water and the flesh becomes soft and pappy. But if you live at the sea (as I do) and carry a dozen mackerel straight up from the harbor and eat them within the hour, you have a dish that is fit for a king.

BROILED MACKEREL

  2 *mackerel* (*gutted*)
  Coarse salt
  Black pepper

Since mackerel are much plumper than herrings, you should make 3 cuts diagonally across the flesh on both sides to allow the heat to penetrate when you go to broil them, 5 minutes a side, then season. (They don't look so pretty when fried, as the skin breaks up a lot.) 2 *servings.*
  Mackerel fillet very well. You can broil or fry the fillets. The English eat gooseberry sauce with mackerel. Not me.

COLD MACKEREL

  Mackerel boiled in sea water for 10 minutes and eaten cold with mayonnaise is delicious.

MACKEREL IN CIDER

  2 *mackerel*
  1½ cups cider
  Salt and pepper

Steep the mackerel in the cider overnight. (The acid in the cider counteracts the oil in the fish.) Dry the fish, make 3 diagonal gashes on each side, and broil. Season and serve. 2 *servings.*
  Or bake in the oven in fresh cider and seasoning.

Lobster

Up to a few years ago lobsters were only a modest luxury in Ireland. You could buy a fine lobster for under a dollar, and if you bought two you could drive a harder bargain. But now the price has gone to high heaven. Airplanes take off from Shannon every morning stacked high with lobsters for the great restaurants of Europe.

The perfect lobsters should come straight from the lobster pots, which the fishermen have set in the morning and harvested the same evening. If lobsters are held in artificial tanks for any length of time they waste inside the shell and the flesh becomes stringy. The true test of quality in a live lobster is that the brute should feel surprisingly heavy for his size when you lift him. (Mind he doesn't take the hand off you.) When you cook him he should have full claws and plenty of creamy meat inside his waistcoat. This is the loveliest part of a lobster and is found only in fish that are freshly taken from their natural feeding grounds. The only inedible parts of a lobster are the thread of gut that runs down the tail and the stomach sac at the head.

Since few Irish housewives would think of buying lobsters, (except live ones that they had poked and prodded on the quayside and held in their hand to judge the weight), there is no tradition of elaborate lobster cuisine in Ireland. We boil them, we broil them, we bake them. We add nothing to them except salt. We wouldn't dare. Think of their *unique* flavor—and think of the price!

COLD BOILED LOBSTER

2 1-pound lobsters
1 pot sea water or 1 pot boiling water with 1 tablespoon salt
and a handful of edible seaweed if available.

Plunge the live lobsters into the salted boiling water, having first tied their claws, otherwise they will fight. Put a tight lid on top and boil for 10 minutes. Remove from water and cool.

Cooking a lobster in water that has been flavored with vegetables and herbs is nonsense. It does nothing whatever for the fish.

When the lobsters are cold, split them in two, crack the claws, remove gut and sac, and present on a bed of lettuce with mayonnaise on the side. *2 servings.*

BROILED LOBSTER

1 lobster weighing 1½ to 2 pounds
Butter
Salt

Kill the lobster by plunging a sharp knife into the cross at the head. The brain (I am told) is behind this. Now split right down the center into two halves. Remove the sac that is near the head, and the thread of gut. Crack the claws to allow the heat to penetrate. Paint the shell and claws with melted butter, and spread soft butter over the upturned flesh of the demi-lobsters. Put under the broiler until it begins to color. Add more butter if necessary, and transfer to a moderate oven (350°) for 5 to 7 minutes more to finish cooking. (You can't turn the half lobster on the broiler or all the juice will run out). Cover with greased aluminum foil or wax paper while in the oven to prevent the flesh from drying out.

Sprinkle with coarse salt and serve.

If you have started off with a lobster that is fresh from the lobster pots, you will have that delicious cream in the body of the lobster. Remember, I mentioned it earlier. If there is no cream, blame the fishmonger—not me. *2 servings, maybe.*

ROAST LOBSTER

1 live lobster 1½ to 2 pounds
Olive oil

Kill the lobster by plunging a skewer into the cross on the head. Paint the shell with olive oil. Wrap in aluminum foil and bake in a moderate oven (350°) for 25 minutes. Leave wrapped in the aluminum foil till quite cold. This must be eaten cold. If you try to crack the shell with the soft, hot meat inside it will all squelch out on you. *1–2 servings.*

LOBSTER IN A CRUST

1 live lobster 1½ to 2 pounds
3 cups flour
1 cup (approx.) water

Kill the lobster. Make a stiff paste of the flour and water. Wrap the lobster in the paste and bake in the oven at 350° until the crust is pale brown—about 30 to 35 minutes. Leave to cool in the crust. Then discard the crust and crack the lobster. *1–2 servings.*

All the classic recipes for cooking lobster are readily available in any good cookery book, but, if you can get your lobsters straight from the sea, these simple preparations are very hard to beat.

Crab

In Ireland crabs can be bought for a few cents. I think it is the troublesome preparation that puts people off them. Also, they are ugly and ungainly-looking beasts, and really they have the dowdiest of shells, don't you think?

If you have the good luck to live by the sea, make sure to buy your crabs alive, and straight out of the water. Those unhappy crabs that you sometimes see crawling drunkenly around a fishmonger's window are often quite useless. They have been wasting and dehydrating in this uncongenial milieu, and when you come to cook them you may find that there is no meat left in the shell.

BOILED CRAB

2 *live crabs*	1 *pot boiling water*
1 *tablespoon salt*	1 *tablespoon vinegar*

Plunge the live crabs into a pot of boiling salted water to which you have added the vinegar. Boil for 25 to 30 minutes, according to size. Remove from the water and allow to get quite cold before attempting to dress them. By the way, the best crabs to buy are those of medium size. Small crabs are not worth the trouble and excessively large ones are often hollow and useless. A good crab should feel heavy when you pick it up in your hand. The female is more delicate in flavor than the male.

If you have never sundered a crab, it is difficult to explain how it is done. A crab is made up of two parts. There is the flat, outside shell with the fluting around the edges, and there is the functional part of the body, to which the legs and claws are attached. This we will call the undercarriage, and it fits as snugly into the shell as only God (and the Rolls-Royce Company) can arrange these things. But you can wrench the body from the shell in the same way as you would pull a reluctant electric plug from a tight-fitting socket. If it won't pull apart, stand the crab on its head and press the other end firmly with your hand. This will break the connection and the two parts will come apart more easily.

When the crab is disjointed, discard the pointed gray ruffle that goes around the edge (this is called "dead man's fingers") and the little sac up at the head (that is the stomach). All the meat in the shell can be eaten, and anything you can poke out of the body with the back of a spoon. Also all the meat in the claws. *4 servings.*

CREAMED CRAB

½ pound picked crab meat
2 tomatoes, peeled and
  chopped
2 hard-boiled eggs, chopped
Chopped parsley

½ cup mayonnaise
¼ cup cream
2 teaspoons vinegar
Salt and pepper

Mix all together and serve on a bed of crisp lettuce.

Serve it as a first course for lunch, or use it to fill tiny *bouchées* of pastry as a cocktail snack. *3–4 servings.*

CRAB IN CHEESE SAUCE

2 tablespoons butter
2 tablespoons flour
1 cup boiling milk
½ pound crab meat
½ cup grated Parmesan
  or any other sharp
  cooking cheese

Pepper
½ teaspoon prepared
  mustard
½ tablespoon lemon juice
½ cup cream

Make a sauce, i.e., melt the butter, add the flour, gradually add the boiling milk. Cook for 10 minutes. Add all other ingredients except 1 tablespoon of the cheese. Taste for saltiness, as cheese is unpredictable. Pour into an ovenproof dish, dust with the reserved cheese, and brown under the broiler. *3–4 servings.*

Dublin Bay Prawns

In Ireland we are fiercely proud of our Dublin Bay prawns, and we prize them far more than lobsters. The flesh is sweet and very tender, and it has that wonderful sea taste. The PRAWN COCK-TAIL is one of our celebrated national delicacies.

PRAWNS WITH MAYONNAISE

> *1 pound live prawns*   *1 tablespoon salt*
> *4 cups boiling water*   *3 tablespoons mayonnaise*
> *1 wide saucepan*

Bring the salted water to a boil in a wide saucepan. Throw in the prawns and, when the water comes to a boil again, poach the prawns for 1 minute. Remove from the water and let the fish get cold. To shell the prawns, pull the tail from the waistcoat. Cut along the underbelly of the tail shell with a sharp scissors and the tail flesh is revealed. (Sounds very complicated, but you would understand if you had a prawn in front of you.) Remove the tail flesh and discard the thread of gut. Serve on a bed of lettuce with mayonnaise. *3 servings.*

Scallops

When you buy sea scallops from the fishmonger, make sure that he gives you the deep, fluted shells as well as the fish. They are so pretty for serving the finished scallops in, and the flat shells are quite useless. Do not discard the orange tongue. That is the coral.

SCALLOPS IN MUSHROOM SAUCE

8 medium sea scallops
1 bay leaf
Salt and pepper
½ cup milk
1 onion
2 tablespoons butter

2 tablespoons flour
½ cup cream
1 clove garlic, crushed
½ tablespoon Irish whiskey
¼ pound small mushrooms
Browned breadcrumbs

Simmer the scallops, bay leaf, salt and pepper in milk for 5 minutes. Remove the scallops and cut into 4 or 5 slices. Strain the milk and reserve.

Melt the chopped onion in butter. Now add flour, stir well. Gradually add heated milk and cream, crushed garlic, and whiskey. Cook for 5 minutes. Lastly, add chopped mushrooms and sliced scallops. Butter 4 deep scallop shells and divide the mixture among them. Top with breadcrumbs and dots of butter and brown under the broiler. *4 servings.*

SCALLOPS WITH CHEESE SAUCE

8 sea scallops
½ cup milk or dry white
   wine
2 tablespoons butter
2 tablespoons flour
A pinch of dry mustard
1 clove garlic, crushed

½ cup grated Parmesan
   or any other sharp
   cooking cheese
½ cup cream
2 egg yolks
Pepper
1 tablespoon grated cheese
   for dusting

Poach the scallops in milk (or wine) for 5 minutes. Remove them from liquid and cut into slices. Reserve liquid. Make a sauce by melting the butter and adding the flour and mustard. Gradually add the reserved liquid and crushed garlic. Cook the sauce for 5 minutes. Remove it from the fire and add the cheese and cream. Beat in the egg yolks. Add the sliced scallops and the pepper. Taste for salt. Divide mixture among 4 buttered scallop shells. Dust over with grated cheese and brown under the broiler. *4 servings.*

Small scallops are very nice dipped in batter and fried in deep fat. They are also very nice raw, straight out of the shell, but you would need to live adjacent to the salt sea before you would risk them.

Cockles and Mussels (Alive, Alive—O!)

In Dublin's fair city, where the girls are so pretty, there was a time when cockles and mussels were sold in great quantities from the stalls on the streets. That custom has gone this many a day, but the old song remains to haunt us like the ghost of Sweet Molly Malone.

In Ireland mussels are looked upon as the poor man's oysters. They are sold at around a dollar for 10 pounds when they are in season. But most of the weight is in the shell, so you really haven't that many mussels when you boil them down.

MUSSEL STEW

10 pounds mussels in the
  shells
1 large onion, chopped
1 tablespoon butter
½ cup water or dry white
  wine

2 cloves garlic, crushed
Pepper
1 tablespoon chopped
  parsley
1 tablespoon extra butter
  for thickening (optional)

Scrub the mussels under running water with a hard-bristled brush, making sure to discard any mussel with an open shell.

Rinse in several waters to remove all the sand. This is most important, as you will otherwise end up with a gritty stew. (When I first cooked mussels I scraped off the little barnacles with a potato peeler and scraped half the skin off my hand in the process. I have long since dispensed with this refinement.)

Melt the chopped onion in the butter. Add the mussels and all the other ingredients except the parsley and the extra butter. No salt, please, for the mussels themselves are quite salty. Put the saucepan on a fierce heat and cover with a glass plate so that you can see when the mussels open. It takes only about 5 minutes. When they are open they are cooked. Fish them out of the liquid and discard the empty top shell and the beard, keeping the shell to which the mussel is attached for serving.

You will be amazed at how much liquid there is now in the pot. The mussels have, on opening, released all their juice. Return this liquid to the heat and let it reduce by fast boiling with the lid off. Add a few lumps of butter to the soup to thicken it, or, if you think that makes it too rich, fortify it with a smooth sauce. But remember, this soup should not be any thicker than a thin cream.

THICKENING SAUCE:

   1 tablespoon butter
   1 tablespoon flour
   ½ cup strained mussel juice
   ½ cup thin cream

Melt butter. Add flour. Cook together for 1 minute. Gradually add mussel juice and cream. Cook together for 5 minutes. Add to soup and boil up.

When the soup is ready, pour it over the half-shelled mussels and garnish with chopped parsley. This is always served in soup plates. *8 servings.*

MUSSELS WITH RICE

6 pounds mussels in the
shell
1 cup rice

1 tablespoon butter
2 cups mussel juice

Cook mussels as in previous recipe until the shells open. Discard both shells and beards and hold the mussels aside. Keep the mussel juice.

Gently fry the rice in butter until the grains are translucent. Add the mussel juice. Bring to a boil and cover with a tight lid. Simmer gently for a half-hour. Add the shelled mussels to the hot rice and garnish with grated Parmesan cheese or tomato sauce. *4 servings.*

Oysters

You will notice that I have included no recipe for cooking oysters. To tell the truth, I never cooked an oyster in my life. They are far too expensive in Ireland to use in the kitchen. They are always eaten raw on the half shell, resting on a plate of cracked ice, with brown bread and butter, lemon wedges, and Irish stout on the side. But, for you fortunate Americans, who have oysters galore, here is a tip. Next time you make a meat stew throw a few oysters in for good measure. They do make such a difference, I promise you.

Sorry I can't tell you how to open oysters. Women never open them in Ireland. It is considered unfeminine, like playing football or smoking a pipe. Anyhow it is frightfully troublesome and is better left to a strong-armed man. You would probably splinter your beautiful fingernails.

MEATS

Dá ghoire dhon chnáimh an fheoil is amhlaidh is milse í.

(The nearer the bone the sweeter the meat.)

Beef

IRELAND has always been famous for the excellence of her beef cattle. We export them all over Europe and we do a roaring trade in pedigree bulls to the four corners of the earth. Indeed, despite the modern trend toward industrialization, Ireland would be put to the pin of her collar to balance her economy were it not for her thriving cattle trade.

With us butter and milk are heavily subsidized by the Government, so that farmers will go on keeping cows that will go on producing delectable, brown-eyed bullocks for the tables of Europe.

Oddly enough, there is no tradition of veal cooking in Ireland —and there is a simple explanation for this. Since we have such an abundance of lush pastureland, there is no economic necessity to kill off the young calf. There is plenty of grass around to feed him until he reaches the maturity of a prime bullock. Even when calves are slaughtered for the table, they have often passed their baby days and are big enough for their minds to turn to thoughts of love. And that is not the way to get choice veal. Never mind, wouldn't you rather have a good steak any day of the week?

Since all the Americans I ever met cook both roast beef and steak to perfection I offer my suggestions with a certain timidity.

By the way, in case I forget to mention it anywhere else, a *baron of beef* and a *sirloin* owe their noble titles to the English King Henry VIII. Henry was a gargantuan eater, and one of his favorite dishes was a good haunch of roast beef.

On one occasion, a particularly appetizing saddle of beef, hot from the spit, was placed in front of him. Flushed with wine, he laid his sword upon it and, good-humoredly, knighted it on the spot. For ever afterward that particular cut came to be known as the *baron,* and the thick slice cut from it was called *Sir Loin.*

ROAST BEEF

1 4-pound sirloin or rib roast	Dry mustard
1 carrot	2 tablespoons beef drippings
1 onion	

Preheat the oven to 400°. Smear the joint lightly with mustard. Put it into the roasting pan with the whole onion, the carrot, and the drippings. Baste with the hot fat after 20 minutes. Reduce the heat to 350° after a half-hour. It is cooked after 45 to 50 minutes. Allow the joint to set on a dish in the kitchen for 10 minutes before carving. The mustard helps to seal in the juice. The onion and carrot help to flavor the gravy. *8-plus servings.*

GRAVY:

Gently pour the fat off the pan without disturbing the sediment. Sprinkle a little flour on the pan and mix it well in with the sediment. Allow this to color and gradually add stock, or cold tea, or the water in which potatoes or vegetables were boiled. Cook for 5 minutes, season, and strain.

TOP RIB

The top rib (the cut just below the shoulder) is also known in Ireland as the "housekeeper's cut." It is an economical joint because it is very lean, but it is tougher than sirloin or ribs. If it is very well hung it makes an excellent family joint when roasted and eaten cold. Cook it as for sirloin, but do not cut it until it is quite cold. The same thing applies to the sirloin. If you want a choice cold joint for supper, do not be tempted to cut a few slices when the joint is hot, or you may let half the juice escape.

If you are a clever carver, you would get 8 servings out of a 4-pound roast.

STEAK AND ONIONS

The only way to get a fillet steak out of a butcher in Ireland is to marry him—and there aren't enough butchers to lead up the aisle. You are more fortunate in America, because if you pay the price you can call the cut. Then again, many people prefer a sirloin. It may not melt under the knife like a fillet, but it has more flavor and a firmer texture.

The ideal way to cook steak is over charcoal. That way, the outside is crisp and brown and the inside is red and spongy. In Ireland, the charcoal broiler is a luxury, so I cook my steak, resting on a wire grid, over a clear turf fire on the hearth in the sitting room. The smoke goes up the chimney and the steak is just as nice as if one had the most elaborate barbecue.

1 *sirloin steak about 4 to 4½ pounds*	1 *teaspoon butter*
1 *clove garlic*	4 *onions, sliced*
1 *tablespoon butter*	*Seasoning for onions*

Crush the garlic in the *teaspoon* of butter. Rub this over the steak, which should be 1½ to 2 inches thick. Do *not* salt the steak, as this draws out the juice. Put it under a hot broiler or over a charcoal broiler. Cook for 7 to 8 minutes a side.

While the steak is cooking, melt the *tablespoon* of butter in a saucepan, add the sliced onions and seasoning. Stir around to absorb the butter and cook gently with the lid on the pan until soft. Serve around the broiled steak as a garnish and rub a pat of butter over the steak to make it shiny.

Carve the steak by cutting it in thick slices along the grain of the meat. Give a good slice of the fillet to your most important male guest (all men are knowledgeable about steak—all that expense-account eating, I'm sure) and never you mind about his wife. The chances are she is so delighted to be away from her own kitchen stove she won't mind what she gets.   *4–6 servings.*

P.S. Cooking the complete steak is far smarter than having six individual cuts. Less trouble, too, and looks more extravagant. Besides, if you are clever with the knife you might be able to feed seven or eight with a little sleight of hand.

STEAK AND KIDNEY STEW

When you make a steak and kidney stew always buy the shin of beef. That is the part near the ankle of the beast. It requires long, slow cooking but it positively melts in the mouth.

2 pounds boned shin of beef
½ pound beef kidney or 2 sheep's kidneys
2 onions, sliced
2 tablespoons flour
Salt and pepper
1 sprig thyme
1 tablespoon chopped parsley
1 cup water
6 to 12 oysters (optional)

Cut the meat in large cubes. Slice the kidney. Toss the meat, kidney, and onion in the seasoned flour. Put into a casserole with the thyme and parsley. Add water. Cover the lot with a piece of aluminum foil, which you press down over the stew. Now put on a tight lid and cook in a moderate oven (300°) for 1½ hours. Add the oysters, stir the stew, and cook for a further hour at 250°. If the stew is too thick you can add a little boiling water. Remove the thyme and dust the stew with chopped parsley before serving. Nice with boiled baby carrots or peas. *6 servings.*

CORNED BEEF AND CABBAGE

This is a very popular dish in Ireland, where all the cheaper cuts of meat are pickled, as butchers find it very difficult to sell them otherwise. We have two main cuts: the brisket, which is a mixture of fat and lean, and the silverside, which is all lean. They are both cooked in the same way. The brisket is sweeter but more wasteful.

4 pounds corned beef	Pepper
Cold water	2 onions
1 sprig thyme, 1 bunch	1 whole carrot
parsley, bound together	1 2-pound cabbage
1 onion stuck with 6 cloves	

Tie the beef into a neat shape. Put it into a large pot and cover with cold water. (No salt, please.) Add all the other ingredients except the cabbage and bring very slowly to a boil, with the lid off the pot so that you can see what is happening. Simmer very gently for 3 hours. Skim when a scum rises. Remove the thyme, parsley, and cloved onion. Now add the cabbage, which has been cut in quarters and well washed in salted cold water. Simmer for a further 20 minutes, or until the cabbage is cooked.

Remove the meat and cut the string. Strain the cabbage, pepper well, and serve on a dish surrounding the beef. *6–8 servings.*

P.S. If the corned beef water is too salty, cook the cabbage in separate water, adding 3 cups of the beef stock to salt and flavor it.

IRISH SPICED BEEF

Around Christmas all the butcher shops in Ireland come out with a positive rash of spiced beef. You will see it (looking like a bundle of soft chocolate) tied up in red ribbon and decorated with holly. After the festive season it disappears completely, never to be seen again until the following December.

You can, however, prepare spiced beef yourself.

TO SPICE BEEF AT HOME

7 pounds brisket, round steak, or tail end of beef, boned

SPICING:

3 shallots	½ teaspoon chopped thyme
4 bay leaves	3 tablespoons brown sugar
1 teaspoon powdered cloves	2 teaspoons potassium
1 teaspoon powdered mace	nitrate
½ teaspoon crushed	1 pound coarse salt
peppercorns	4 tablespoons molasses
1 teaspoon allspice	

Chop the shallots and bay leaves very finely. Mix all the dry ingredients together and add the shallots and bay leaves. Stand the meat in a large pan and rub the mixture well into it on all sides. Leave the meat resting on this aromatic bed for 2 days. Now pour the molasses over it and rub the mixture well into the meat every day for 1 week. At the end of that time, tie the meat into a neat shape. Cover well with warm water and simmer gently for 6 hours. Press between 2 dishes with a weight on top. This is always eaten cold. *12 servings.*

PRESSED BEEF TONGUE

1 pickled beef tongue
12 cloves
1 pot cold water

When you buy a pickled tongue, make sure that the butcher does not cut away the bone at the back of the throat. This makes the jelly that enables the tongue to set when you come to press it.

Steep the tongue for 4 to 5 hours to remove excessive salt.

Put in a pot and cover well with cold water. Add the cloves. Bring slowly to a boil and simmer for 4 hours. Leave the tongue in the water until it is cool enough to handle (about the temperature of a hot bath). Take out the tongue. Put it in a wide dish to capture the juices. Peel off the skin and cut away the bone at the throat. You will also find some tiny bones embedded in the flesh at the back. Remove these too with a searching finger.

Now curl the tongue in a circle and put it into a 6-inch saucepan (or a cake pan) where it will fit tightly. Add the juice that has come out of the tongue (this makes the jelly). Put a small plate that fits *inside* the saucepan on top, and a heavy weight on top of that. Leave it overnight in the refrigerator to set. If you have difficulty in turning the tongue out of the container, plunge the vessel in hot water for a few seconds, and the round tongue will come out easily.

To serve, slice the tongue across the circle. Very economical —and so delicate. *12 servings.*

IRISH BEEF TEA

This is really invalid cooking and is far too troublesome for the hale and hearty. It was a great favorite with my grandmother, who lived until she was as old as a field. She always added a little whiskey to it to give her added nourishment. The great thing about beef tea is that the flavor is so mild (no onions, no herbs) that the sick can drink it when anything more pungent would cause nausea.

½ pound lean steak
1 cup water
1 pinch salt

Scrape the meat with a sharp knife to remove all the meat cells. The white fiber that holds the cells together is discarded. The

red cells are put into a jam jar, together with the water and salt.
Cover the jar and stand it in a deep saucepan containing enough
water to come three-quarters way up the sides of the jar. Infuse
on a low heat on top of the stove for 6 to 7 hours, or put it into
a slow oven for the same time. Strain and serve after removing
any grease that may be on top. *1 serving.*

Lamb

By their very nature sheep were designed to thrive in mountain-
ous districts and on poor land. The best sheep in Ireland are to
be found in Connemara, in the Aran Islands, and in the more
rugged parts of Kerry. They live on the short, salty grass that is
sprayed by the Atlantic foam, and their flesh has a sweetness
not to be found in animals reared on more luxuriant pastures.

With us, the first lamb appears in the shops at Easter when
it is the traditional Easter Sunday dinner. It is the harbinger of
spring, when the sap is again rising in the trees, when a young
man's fancy turns to thoughts of love, when summer is nigh.

ROAST LEG OF LAMB

1 clove garlic	10 to 12 parsley stalks
1 tablespoon butter	1 carrot
1 leg of lamb, 4 to 5	1 onion
pounds	1 tablespoon water

Crush the garlic and mix with the butter. Paint the leg with the
garlic butter and lay it in the roasting pan, resting on the parsley
stalks, with the carrot, the onion, and the water. Roast it at
350°, reducing the heat toward the end of the cooking time.
Allow 20 minutes to the pound and 20 minutes over. Baste when
you think of it. The idea of the carrot and onion is to add interest
to the gravy. *8 servings and more.*

GRAVY:

The sediment from the
   roasting pan
1 tablespoon flour
Carrot and onion from the
   roast

1 tablespoon mint jelly
1¼ cups beef stock or
   cold tea
Salt and pepper

Gently pour the fat off the roasting pan without disturbing the sediment. Sprinkle in the flour. Mix well with the sediment and allow to brown. Add the mashed, cooked carrot and onion and the jelly. Gradually add stock or cold tea. Cook for 5 minutes. Season and strain.

ROAST LEG OF LAMB IN A CRUST

1 leg of lamb, 5 to 6
   pounds
1 clove garlic, crushed
5 cups flour

1½ cups (approx.) cold
   water
1 tablespoon butter

Rub the joint with the crushed garlic. Make a stiff paste of the flour and water. Roll this out and cover the leg completely with the paste. Put it into an ungreased roasting pan and bake at 350°, allowing 25 minutes to the pound. Reduce heat if crust browns too fast.

Crack the paste and discard. Put the joint back in the oven, well painted with soft butter, and bake until lightly browned. *10 servings.*

BOILED LEG OF LAMB AND PARSLEY SAUCE

1 leg of lamb, 5 to 6 pounds	2 onions
	2 stalks celery
Enough boiling water to cover	2 leeks
1 bunch parsley	2 cloves garlic
1 sprig thyme	1 bay leaf
2 carrots	1 cup barley
	2 teaspoons salt

When the water is boiling, add the lamb and all the other ingredients except the salt. Bring slowly to a boil again and simmer gently for 2 hours. Skim if necessary from time to time. Add salt and simmer for another half-hour. Turn off the heat and let the leg set in the water while you make the sauce.

PARSLEY SAUCE:

1½ cups finely chopped parsley	3 tablespoons flour
1 cup milk	1 cup of the strained cooking liquid
3 tablespoons butter	Salt and pepper

Boil the chopped parsley in the milk for 1 minute. Melt the butter, add the flour, and cook together for 2 minutes. Gradually add the boiling parsley-milk and the hot cooking liquid as you stir, taking care not to cause lumps. Season and cook for 10 minutes.

Pour over the leg of lamb and serve. *10 servings.*

Next day remove the caked fat from the liquid in which the lamb was boiled. Discard the tired vegetables. Add fresh soup vegetables, which have been neatly chopped. Boil for 20 minutes, or until the new vegetables are cooked, and you have a delicious broth. The barley gives it a nice body.

By the way, boiled leg of lamb is a great favorite with most men.

ROAST SHOULDER OF LAMB

    1 shoulder of lamb, 3½   1 sprig rosemary
       to 4½ pounds   1 onion
    1 tablespoon butter or   1 carrot
       lamb drippings   1 tablespoon water

Lay the buttered shoulder on a bed of rosemary. Add the onion, carrot, and water. Bake at 350° for 1½ hours, basting from time to time. *8 servings at least.*

LAMB STEW

    2 pounds lean neck of   2 cloves garlic
       lamb   1 sprig thyme
    2 onions   1 bunch parsley
    2 tablespoons flour   1 cup water
    Salt and pepper   ¼ pound small mushrooms
    1½ tablespoons butter   ½ cup evaporated milk

Disjoint the lamb. Slice the onions. Toss in the seasoned flour and fry lightly in the butter. Put the meat and onions in a casserole with the garlic, thyme, and parsley, then add the water. Press wax paper down over the meat and cover the casserole with a tight lid. Cook in a moderate oven (350°) for 1½ hours. Discard the thyme and parsley. Add the mushrooms, stir, and cook a further 20 minutes or until the meat is tender. Remove fat, if any, stir well, and enrich with the hot evaporated milk.

This is a blond stew and will need bright-colored vegetables, like young peas or carrots, to accompany it. *4 servings.*

LAMB LIVER

1 pound lamb liver
1 pinch mixed herbs
Pepper
1 tablespoon flour
1 tablespoon butter

Extra butter
Lemon juice
Chopped parsley
Salt

Slice the liver in half-inch thicknesses. Mix the herbs and pepper in the flour and toss the liver in this. Melt the butter in a heavy pan. Fry the liver in this. Remove the liver to a hot dish. Wipe the pan. Add more butter, the lemon juice, and chopped parsley. When melted pour over the liver, salt, and serve. *4 servings.*

Don't overcook the liver—it should be pink inside.

LAMB KIDNEYS IN THEIR JACKETS

6 lamb kidneys encased in their jackets of fat

Put the kidneys (in their fatty jackets) in a hot oven (400°) and roast for 25 minutes, or until fat is translucent. Remove the fat casing and serve on buttered toast.

This was a great favorite with my father, who would eat all 6 baby kidneys for breakfast. It is simply lovely—and so easy. *2 servings.*

LAMB SWEETBREADS

The sweetbreads are at their best in the early part of the lamb season.

1 *pound lamb sweetbreads* 1 *tablespoon flour*
2 *cups cold water* 1 *tablespoon butter*
1 *pinch mixed herbs* 3 *lemon wedges*
Salt and pepper

Put the sweetbreads in a pan of cold water and bring slowly to a boil. Cook for 10 minutes. Refresh them in cold water. Cut away all gristle and membrane. Add the herbs and seasoning to the flour. Toss the sweetbreads in this and fry in the butter till lightly browned. Serve with lemon wedges. *3 servings.*

LAMB HEADS

There is only one thing likely to put you off cooking lamb heads, and that is the look of them. They are so sad, with their tiny little skulls and their eyeless sockets. But they make very good broth and the flesh around the cheeks is the most delicate part of the lamb. You also have the tongues and the brains. In Ireland they cost almost nothing.

LAMB BRAINS

2 *lamb heads* ½ *tablespoon flour*
Water *Salt and pepper*
½ *tablespoon vinegar* ½ *tablespoon butter*

The butcher will cleave the heads down the center. Remove the brains. Soak them in several waters to remove the blood. Poach gently for 10 minutes in a pot of water to which you have added the vinegar. When cold, slice them and toss in the seasoned flour. Fry them in butter until lightly browned.

They have an interesting, chalky taste. Besides, there is a curious fascination about eating brains—a commodity we could all do with more of. *1 serving.*

LAMB TONGUES AND CHEEKS

2 *lamb heads*	1 *carrot*
W*ater*	1 *bunch parsley*
1 *onion*	*Salt and pepper*

Steep the cloven lamb heads (minus the brains) in several waters to remove the blood. Put them in a pot of cold water with all the other ingredients. Bring them slowly to a boil and simmer for 1 hour. Skim several times. When the liquid is still warm remove the heads. Cut out the tongues and skin them. Take the soft flesh from the cheeks. Put the tongues and flesh into a small bowl with 2 teaspoons of the juice. Put a coffee saucer on top and weight it down. (You can use the stock as a basis for soup.)

Naturally, you will say this is a lot of trouble for so little reward, but, if you have a family to feed on a small budget, you might do worse.

IRISH STEW

The original Irish stew was made, not from mutton, but from kid. In those far-off days sheep were too valuable to put in the pot for the poor man's family dinner, but young male kids had little value except for their skins. These were peeled off and dried and sold for a few pence. The flesh was used in a stew.

I can still remember my great-grandmother, an old, old woman, bent in two with rheumatism, making a traditional Irish stew in the old-fashioned bastable oven in her cottage kitchen. The bastable oven was a large black pot about eighteen inches in diameter. It was covered with a flat iron lid that had a small handle in the center. At the side of the pot there were two lugs to receive the iron arms that came down from a crook in the chimney. There were three stumpy feet on the pot so that it could stand, when occasion demanded, at the side of the hearth. This pot served many purposes. It was used for an Irish stew, for roasting a fowl or a piece of meat, and for baking the bread.

The pot was suspended by the crooks over the turf fire and glowing red sods were put on top of the lid to give extra heat from above. No modern gadget that has since been made has ever equaled this simple peasant utensil for preserving the true flavor of bread and meat.

3 pounds neck of lamb	1 sprig thyme
12 medium potatoes	2 cups (approx.) water
4 large onions, sliced	Salt and pepper

Remove the fat from the meat and cut into 8 to 10 sections through the bone. Do not remove the bone, as this adds flavor. Peel the potatoes and slice one-third of them in thin slices. Leave the rest of the potatoes whole.

Into a saucepan put the thinly sliced potatoes, then a layer of sliced onions, and then the sections of lamb. Season well. Add the thyme and another layer of sliced onion. Cover with the remainder of the potatoes, which have been left whole. Season again and add 2 cups of water. Cover the pot with aluminum foil and with a very tight-fitting lid.*

Cook in the oven for 2½ hours at 350° or simmer gently over the stove for the same time.

The thinly sliced potatoes at the bottom of the pot should

* In the old days in Ireland the stew was first covered with a thick paste of flour and water to seal in the steam. Then the lid was placed on top. When the stew was cooked the paste was thrown to the hens and the stew was eaten with great relish. There is a vulgar version of this stew in which carrots are added. Very wrong.

dissolve and thicken the juice, while the potatoes on top retain their shape and remain floury. This stew is very easy on the digestion. *6 servings.*

TRIPE AND ONIONS

Since in Ireland tripe is the stomach lining of a sheep, it seems sensible to put it in along with lamb. Tripe is a curious thing—you either love it or you can't stand the sight of it. There is no tolerant middle course. But, you know, it has a lot to recommend it. It is cheap, it has a silky texture and it is so good for you. One of the kindest of dishes for a temperamental digestion. Children should be introduced to tripe when they are very young, because it is an acquired taste and the sooner they acquire it the better.

3 pounds honeycomb tripe	*Salt and pepper*
4 cups milk	*2 tablespoons butter*
4 medium onions, sliced	*3 tablespoons flour*
1 bay leaf	*4 slices of bacon*

Wash the tripe and simmer in salted water for 2 hours. Refresh in cold water. Cut the tripe in generous pieces. Put into a saucepan with the milk, sliced onions, bay leaf, and seasonings. Cook gently for 1 hour.

Melt the butter in another saucepan. Add the flour and cook for 1 minute. Strain the milk off the tripe and add this to the butter-flour to make a smooth sauce. Add the tripe and onions to the sauce (throw away the bay leaf) and cook gently for a further 15 minutes. Broil the bacon. Cut it up finely and add to the tripe. The crisp bacon gives a bite to this bland dish. *4–6 servings.*

NOTE: You should save the rinds of bacon; when you have a reasonable amount put them in a roasting pan in a hot oven until they are curled and crisp. Crumble them and store in a covered jar in the refrigerator. Wonderful scattered over tripe or cooked cauliflower. Such a nice crunch under your teeth.

Pork

What a wonderful animal is the pig—dead, I mean. You would never fall in love with a live pig, and he can be a marauder, too. We once had a pig that ate ducks. But a dead pig is a different matter altogether. Think of the crackling of roast pork, the sweet taste of spareribs, a pink ham, sausages, the breakfast bacon, a shimmering brawn.

When I was young we used to kill our own pigs and cure our own bacon. If I shut my eyes, I can still hear the piercing scream of the pig—like the screech of a jet taking off—as he met his end in the hay barn. For days afterward mother occupied the whole of the kitchen table making puddings from the blood and salting down the sides in crocks. Thank heaven, women are no longer expected to go in for these refinements. Where would you find a man nowadays who would dare lay a dead pig on the kitchen table? And wouldn't you shoot him if he dared?

ROAST PORK

A *cut of pork, 4 to 5 pounds, from the hind leg*	1 *tablespoon bacon drippings*
6 *parsley stalks*	1 *cup water*
	1 *cooking apple*

With a sharp knife score the skin around the joint so that this will afterward produce the crackling and also make the joint easier to carve. Push a few short parsley stalks into the pink flesh with your thumb. Rub the bacon drippings into the scored skin to encourage it to crisp. Put the joint in the roasting pan with the water and the whole apple. Bake in a hot oven (400°), allowing 35 minutes to the pound. Reduce the heat in the last hour. These joints take 2½ to 3 hours. The water helps to keep the joint moist. If it dries up, add more. *10 servings.*

STUFFED PORK STEAK

This is a speciality of County Cork, where Henry Ford's family originally came from.

> 2 *pork steaks*
> 2 *tablespoons butter* or *bacon drippings*

STUFFING:

1 *onion*	1 *teaspoon mixed herbs*
2 *tablespoons butter*	*Salt and pepper*
2 *cups white breadcrumbs*	½ *cup water*
½ *cup chopped parsley*	1 *egg, beaten*

For the stuffing, chop the onion and brown lightly in half the butter. Add to a bowl containing the breadcrumbs, parsley, herbs, and seasoning. Add the rest of the melted butter, the water, and enough of the beaten egg to moisten.

(Now I must explain about the pork steaks, because they may have another name altogether in America. What *we* call a pork steak is the long strip of flesh that lies on either side of the lumbar region. It is the choicest cut in the pig and is equivalent to the fillet in a bullock. It is never pickled—much too delicate for that.)

Slit the steaks along the length, but do not cut through. You want to widen them, but you do *not* want to sever them. Open out the steaks. Lay one steak on the table and lay the stuffing on top. Cover with the second steak, which has also been opened out. Secure the whole with string as if you were tying a parcel.

Plaster well with the butter or bacon drippings. Put in a roasting pan with the water and bake in a hot oven (400°) for 20 minutes. Turn it over, reduce heat to 320°, then bake a further 40 minutes. Baste from time to time. Cover loosely with aluminum foil if the meat is inclined to get too brown. Good hot or cold. *6 servings.*

PORK AND APPLE STEW

6 shoulder pork chops	Salt and plenty of black
4 sour apples of medium	pepper
size	1 tablespoon water
3 onions	
1½ tablespoons brown	
sugar	

Trim the chops of excess fat and cut the fat in thin strips. Peel, core, and slice the apples. Slice the onions thinly. In a wide casserole put a layer of sliced onions, a layer of sliced apples, half the brown sugar, the chops, salt, a generous grinding of black pepper, and the water. Now cover the chops with a layer of onions and a top layer of sliced apples. Toss the strips of pork fat in the other half of the brown sugar. Lay them, crisscross, on top of the apples and throw the remaining sugar over all. Season again with salt and black pepper. Cover the casserole and cook in a moderate oven (350°) for 1 hour. Reduce heat and cook another hour—even more if you want to go out shopping.

This is very good and not half as bothersome as I have made it sound. It is just as good if you put it into the oven at 250° and go off about your business for 3 hours. *3 or 6 servings.*

SKIRTS AND BODICES

These names refer to specialities of County Cork. I bet you'd never guess what skirts and bodices are doing in a section on pork. Hold a moment and I'll tell you. Bodices are the local Cork name for the pickled spareribs, reminiscent of the boned bodices our grandmothers wore. The skirts are the fluted trimmings that are cut away from the pork steaks.

You'll get bodices, all right, in America, but I doubt if you will come across the skirts unless you live in a bacon-curing area. I can't get them even in Dublin.

SKIRTS AND KIDNEYS

2 pork kidneys
2 pounds lean pork
    trimmings or 2 pounds
    shoulder of pork
Salt and pepper
1½ tablespoons flour
1½ tablespoons bacon
    drippings

3 onions
1 cup water
A pinch of herbs
2 parsnips, sliced or 1
    pound pickled spareribs

Cut the kidneys into small pieces and cut the pork in strips. Toss both in the seasoned flour and fry lightly in the drippings. Slice the onions and put in the bottom of the pot with the meats on top. Add the water, herbs, and seasoning and simmer for a half-hour. Add 2 sliced parsnips and continue cooking until all is tender.

Sometimes 1 pound of pickled pork spareribs is added to the stew at the beginning of cooking. Then the parsnips are left out. Traditionally, this dish is eaten with potatoes boiled in their jackets and with parsnips or mashed turnips on the side. 6 servings.

BOILED BACON AND CABBAGE

2 pounds Irish streaky
  bacon (in piece)
1 fresh white cabbage or
  4 young cabbages
  (green)

1 onion
Black pepper
1 tablespoon breadcrumbs
½ tablespoon brown sugar
8 to 10 cloves

Soak the bacon in water for 12 hours. Put in a saucepan and cover well with cold water. Bring slowly to a boil and simmer gently for 1½ hours. It is cooked when the bones come out easily and when the skin pulls off without effort. Turn off the heat and leave the bacon to set in the water while you prepare the cabbage.

CABBAGE:

Cut them in quarters. Wash them well in salted water and rinse in fresh water. Cut out the tough stalks. Plunge cabbage into a pan of fast-boiling water with a skinned onion (this helps to counteract the acrid smell) and boil fast for 5 minutes. Now add 2 to 3 cupfuls of the liquid in which the bacon was cooked. This will salt the cabbage and flavor it. Continue cooking until cabbage is tender but still retains a slight bite. (Almost everybody overcooks cabbage, and that is why it has such a poor reputation.) Drain well and dust with black pepper.

Skin the bacon and cover the back with the breadcrumbs mixed with the sugar. Stud with cloves and brown under the broiler. Slice and serve with the cabbage. *6 servings.*

P.S. In my young days the cabbage was always cooked with the bacon, but at that time bacon was much more mildly cured.

Irish boiled bacon and cabbage is always served with potatoes boiled in their jackets.

HAM

I'll tell you an interesting thing about ham. The true ham epicure (and Ireland is full of them—especially the men) will always look for the left ham of a pig. It is considered more tender and delicate. You see, the pig scratches himself with the right leg and consequently exercises it far more. So it is tougher—well, slightly. Of course, if the pig happens to be left-footed (like I am) this theory goes for nothing.

In traditional Irish cooking the whole ham was always boiled and later covered with sugar and breadcrumbs and studded with cloves. Baking a ham, or a piece of ham, in a crust is a modern refinement. (Americans are wonderful at baking ham with fruit.)

It is my own personal opinion that baked ham is delicious when served hot, but that a slice from a ham that has been boiled is juicier if the joint is cold. (Do you detect a touch of patriotic prejudice here?)

BOILED IRISH HAM

1 ham, 12 pounds
1 quart Irish stout (this is cheap in Ireland)
½ cup sugar
1 wisp of fresh hay (impossible in a city, I know)

Enough cold water to cover the ham
2 tablespoons breadcrumbs
2 tablespoons brown sugar
Cloves

Soak the ham in cold water for 24 hours to soften. Put it into a large pot with the stout, sugar, and hay and add enough cold water to cover the ham. Bring very slowly to a boil and simmer, at the bubble, allowing 20 to 25 minutes to the pound. If the ham is cooked too fast, it will become tough and stringy.

At the end of the cooking time turn off the heat and let the ham set for at least a half-hour in the liquid. Now take it out of the pot and whip off the skin. Cover the fat with the bread-crumbs and sugar mixed together. Stud generously with cloves and return to a hot oven to color.

For cold ham, you should let the joint cool completely in the liquid and do not color in the oven.

The addition of the hay (is your husband a farmer?) makes a sweet country smell in the kitchen.

Don't ever be tempted to cook a whole ham unless you have a large family, or a large party, to eat it up. There is nothing you can get so sick of as slices of cold ham continuing, relent-lessly, through the week.

P.S. If you are cooking a small piece of ham, say 4 pounds, be sure to tie it into a neat shape before lowering it into the liquid. Otherwise it is likely to become quite deformed in the cooking.

BAKED IRISH HAM

> 1 4-pound center cut of ham
> 8 cups flour
> 2½ cups (approx.) water

Soak the ham overnight. (By the way, never remove the bone from ham—it adds so much to the flavor and enables the joint to cook through to the center.) Make a stiff paste of the flour and water and completely envelop the ham in this. Make sure there are no holes or cracks. Bake in a moderate oven (350°) for 2 hours, or until the crust is nicely browned. Allow to cool for a half-hour before removing the crust. Discard the crust.

This is more successful than baking in aluminum foil, though the principle is the same. The protective crust keeps the ham from cooking too fast. *8–10 servings.*

IRISH SAUSAGES

There has always been a great tradition of sausage-making in Ireland, and many of the emigrant Irish now living in England place regular orders with pork butchers in Dublin for a weekly supply of their favorite brand. Among the most celebrated are the Hafners sausages of Dublin and the Hick sausages of Dalkey and Dun Laoghaire. Indeed, no compatriot ever went to see James Joyce in Paris without bringing him 2 pounds of Hafners sausages and a bottle of Powers Irish whiskey.

When Bertie Smyllie, then an excitable young reporter on the *Irish Times,* learned from the news tape that W. B. Yeats had won the Nobel Prize for Poetry in 1923, he phoned the poet to tell him the good news.

"Let me be the first to congratulate you, Mr. Yeats," said Smyllie, bubbling into the phone. "You have won the Nobel Prize."

"How much is it?" asked Yeats.

"Over seven thousand pounds, sir." This represented some $30,500 at the current rate of exchange.

"Splendid, my good man. You must come round and celebrate with us. We are having sausages for tea."

In Ireland sausages are eaten for breakfast, for lunch, for tea, for cocktails, for picnics.

FRIED SAUSAGES

1 pound freshly made sausages
½ tablespoon bacon drippings

Prick the sausages well with a fork to prevent them from bursting in the cooking. Melt the bacon drippings in the pan and put the sausages in. Cover the pan with a loose lid. Turn the sausages from time to time until they are well browned. Cooking time—6 minutes. Drain the sausages on absorbent paper and serve with broiled bacon. *4 servings.*

Or you can broil them.

But it is very important to remember to prick them, especially if the sausages are freshly made by your own pork butcher.

DUBLIN CODDLE

This is a dish that is eaten by families who have lived for generations in Dublin and who look upon the city as their local village. Sean O'Casey ate Dublin coddle and Brendan Behan's mother still makes it. Dean Swift ate it in the Deanery of St. Patrick's Cathedral in the eighteenth century. I must say that I could live without Dublin coddle, but if I thought it would make me write like Dean Swift, I would be quite prepared to lump it and like it.

It is eaten especially on Saturday night when the men come home from the pubs.

1 *pound onions*	*Salt and pepper*
6 *slices of bacon*	1 *cup water*
1 *pound sausages*	

Skin and slice the onions. Put them into a saucepan with the bacon and sausages. Season and add water. Lay wax paper on top. Cover with a tight lid and simmer gently for a half-hour.

This was always washed down by draughts of Irish stout. *6 servings.*

*   *   *

DRISHEENS

Drisheens are another speciality of County Cork. They are made from sheep's blood. In appearance they resemble a blown-up bicycle tire, but they have a wonderful texture, like baked egg custard. Served with melted butter, flavored with tansy, they are an interesting regional dish.

Drisheens are made commercially (on a very small scale) in Cork. I once tried to make them at home but ended up, like Lady Macbeth, dripping in gore.

I only touch on them here because they are unique to Cork. Seán O'Faoláin and Frank O'Connor, both Cork men, would journey home especially for them. But there are many people who can't stand the sight of them.

BLACK AND WHITE PUDDINGS

These are made from pig's blood and, like sausages, are fashioned to family recipes by individual pork butchers. Nobody makes them at home nowadays.

BRAWN

½ pig's head, pickled	3 blades mace
1 pound shin of beef	1 pig's trotter
1 onion stuck with cloves	1 raw beet (optional)
2 bay leaves	8 peppercorns
1 sprig thyme	Crushed black pepper

Put the pig's head in a wide saucepan (if the half head is too big split it in two) with the shin of beef and all the other ingredients. Barely cover with cold water and bring gently to the boil. Simmer for 2 hours. Lift out the meat and the head and strain the stock. Skim off excess fat and reduce by fast boiling.

Pull the meat from the pig's cheek and tear with your fingers into small pieces. Ditto with the shin of beef. Slice the ear into strips. Put all into a mold and add plenty of crushed black pepper. Add enough of the reduced stock to come level with the meat. Cover it with a plate and press down with a weight. Set it in the refrigerator. Next day unmold, slice thinly, and eat with salad. A raw beet added at the beginning gives a rosy color to the brawn.

Don't ever let children see you cooking a pig's head. It will scare the daylights out of them. *8 servings.*

BOILED CRUBEENS (PIG'S FEET)

Crubeens is the Irish name for pig's trotters. There is an interesting thing about pig's feet. The front feet are made up entirely of tiny bones and gristle and are used only to give setting strength to a brawn or a galantine. The hind feet are the true crubeens, which have succulent bits of meat concealed around the bones. At one time they were a great favorite in the pubs of Ireland on a Saturday night, when they were consumed in large numbers. The custom still continues in parts of the South.

I am very proud of the fact that I have been elected the first and only woman Member of Cumann Crubeen na h-Éireann, an exclusive, crubeen-eating club that meets every Saturday night in Tramore, County Waterford. It is like being a Woman Member of the Freemasons!

6 *pig's trotters (from the hind legs)*	12 *peppercorns*
	Salt
1 *onion stuck with 6 cloves*	1 *bunch parsley*
1 *carrot*	1 *sprig thyme*
1 *bay leaf*	

Throw everything into a pot and cover with water. Bring slowly
to a boil and simmer for 3 hours. Eat hot or cold.   2 *servings*.

Crubeens should always be eaten with your fingers. They lose
half their magic if you attack them with a refined knife and fork.
You will need a bath afterward, of course, but their sweet savor
is well worth the extra ablution.

POULTRY AND GAME

Ná díol do chearc lá fluich.

(Never sell your hens on a wet day.)

Chicken

WHEN I was a young girl, chickens were looked upon as a luxury. They were eaten only on Sundays and feast days or when we had very important visitors—and they were always accompanied by a piece of boiled ham or bacon.

Mother was considered very lucky with fowl, and it was a common sight to see seven or eight broody hens wandering around the farmyard, followed by their families of chirruping chickens. At night the chickens would nestle under the warm bodies of the mother hens, and it was a wonder to all of us children that they didn't smother.

Every morning, in spring and summer, we were awakened by the crowing of the cocks. Our hens had a respectable and contented family life and magnificent cock-husbands to cherish them.

In those days chickens *tasted* like chickens and their flesh well deserved its luxury status. But things are different now. With the advent of mass production, and scientific feeding, chickens have lost a lot of their natural flavor.

I remember once seeing a curious sight on our farm. Mother was attempting to make cider from a recipe she found in an old book. She had two barrels of apples steeping in a shed for weeks. When she eventually drew off the cider (which was a complete failure), she threw the sour pulp in the corner of a field. That evening all the hens (and two sows) could be seen reeling around the farmyard, completely drunk. The cocks kept on trying to crow, but the only sounds that came out of them were hoarse croaks. There were hardly any eggs next day. The pigs snored loudly for sixteen hours.

In those days we always killed our own cockerels, plucked them, gutted them, and cooked them immediately. The blood was saved and later seasoned and fried on the pan in sizzling butter. It was delicious. (Goose blood is even nicer.)

Describing a woman of uncertain age, my mother would often say: "She wouldn't tear in the plucking" (young birds have very delicate skin that breaks easily with inept plucking) or: "A chicken of her age wouldn't fall off the roost."

Mother had a tongue that would clip a hedge.

STUFFED ROAST CHICKEN

1 chicken, 4 to 4½
   pounds, with its giblets
2 slices fat bacon

½ cup water
Grated nutmeg

STUFFING:

1 onion
2 tablespoons melted butter
1½ cups white breadcrumbs
2 tablespoons chopped
   parsley

½ teaspoon chopped thyme
1 clove garlic, crushed
Salt and pepper
A little milk if necessary

Chop the onion and fry lightly in the butter. Add this to the
breadcrumbs, parsley, thyme, garlic, and seasonings, which have
been well mixed in a bowl. Bind it with your hand, and if it is
too dry, moisten with a little milk. Put this into the crop of the
bird (the crop is under the flap of skin at the neck). Sew down
the skin over the stuffing. Cover the breast of the chicken with
the fat bacon and secure with string. Put the liver and a little
butter into the belly. Paint the legs and other exposed flesh with
soft butter and lay the bird in the roasting pan, together with the
neck and gizzard. Add a half cup of water to the pan. Cover
loosely with aluminum foil and bake at 350° for 1½ to 2 hours.
In the last half-hour remove the foil and the bacon to let the
bird color, and dust the breast with nutmeg. Serve with BREAD
SAUCE (given below). *4–5 servings.*

BREAD SAUCE:

1 onion	1 cup white breadcrumbs
12 cloves	Salt and pepper
1 small bay leaf	1 teaspoon butter
2 cups milk	1 tablespoon cream

Peel the onion and stud with the cloves. Put the onion and bay leaf into a saucepan and cover with the milk. Let it simmer on a low heat for a half-hour, to draw out the flavor of the onion. Remove the onion and bay leaf. Boil up the milk and add the breadcrumbs. Stir gently to let the breadcrumbs absorb the milk. Reheat. Add seasonings, butter, and cream and serve as soon as possible. This sauce gets pasty if it is left too long.

BOILED CHICKEN
(see CHICKEN AND HAM SOUP)

A boiled chicken that has been left in the liquid to get quite cold and then served with mayonnaise is *much* nicer than cold roast chicken. More moist.

BONED CHICKEN

1 cold boiled chicken about 3½ pounds (see recipe above)	1 large raw chicken 4½ to 5 pounds, boned
¾ pound minced tongue	2 cups rich white masking sauce (given below)
¾ pound minced ham	1 small sprig parsley
Salt and pepper	1 small carrot, boiled
1 truffle	
1 cup aspic jelly (1 tablespoon powdered gelatin dissolved in a cup of chicken stock)	

Remove the cold boiled chicken from the cooking liquid. Cut all the flesh away from the breast, legs, etc., and discard the skin. Mince very finely. Add to the minced tongue and ham and knead together with your hand. Add seasonings, the truffle, cut in neat pieces, and 2 tablespoons of the aspic jelly. Mix well.

Lay the uncooked boned chicken on the table with the skin side down. (I do hope the poulterer will bone the bird for you, as it would take pages to explain the operation.) Roll three-quarters of the minced meats into an oval shape, and with the other quarter stuff the 2 legs where the bones were removed. Tie the ends of the legs to prevent the stuffing from escaping. Lay the oval of stuffing along the center of the raw flesh (this takes the place of the cage of bone). Bring the flesh together over the stuffing. Sew all the way along the back with a bright-colored thread. Now turn the stuffed chicken over and, with your hands, shape it to look like a proper chicken, tucking the legs well in at the sides.

Wrap the bird firmly in muslin and poach gently in chicken stock for 1 hour. Let it get quite cold in the water. Remove the muslin, whip out the bright-colored sewing thread, and put the chicken on a cake rack with a plate underneath.

Mask the chicken completely with the rich white sauce given below. When the sauce has set, decorate the breast of the chicken with a thin stalk of parsley along the center, a few sprigs of parsley leaves, and small rings of boiled carrot on either side. You want the decoration to look like a delicate spray of flowers. I almost forgot to tell you that you should dip this vegetation in the aspic first, so that it will not slip off the chicken. When the decoration has set, mask the lot with the remaining clear aspic jelly, which should be on the point of setting.

Leave the bird in the refrigerator for 12 hours.

To serve, slice it across the body—there is no bone to resist the knife. A circle of white chicken flesh surrounds the pink stuffing.

Very, very troublesome, I know, but very snob. *12 servings.*

MASKING SAUCE:

½ cup milk
2 blades mace
1 bay leaf
2 tablespoons butter
2 tablespoons flour
½ cup strained chicken
   stock

2 tablespoons cream
1 tablespoon of aspic jelly
   (1 tablespoon powdered
   gelatin dissolved in a cup
   of chicken stock)

Infuse the milk with the mace and bay leaf for 15 minutes. Discard the mace and bay leaf. Melt the butter in a saucepan, add flour, and cook for 2 minutes, stirring well. Gradually add the hot milk and chicken stock, stirring all the time. Cook for 10 minutes. Add the cream and aspic jelly. Beat well and use for masking the chicken.

The plate under the cake rack that the chicken is resting on will catch the sauce that runs off. You can spoon it up again. This sauce needs to have the consistency of thick cream. A thin sauce will not stay on the chicken.

STEAMED BREAST OF CHICKEN

The 2 breasts of a
   2½ pound chicken
Butter

1 teaspoon lemon juice
Salt

Fillet the breasts from the chicken. Lightly butter a soup plate. Lay the breasts in it with a little butter and the lemon juice on top. Cover with a lid and put the plate over a pan of fast-boiling water. After 20 minutes, turn the breast in the plate, cover, and cook a further 20 minutes. Salt and serve with its cooking juice.

This is really for invalids. It is more palatable to the sick than chicken that has been boiled and flavored with soup vegetables, and it is far more delicate than roast chick. You will have to eat up the legs yourself. *1–2 servings.*

TINKERS' CHICKEN

In Ireland we have a fair number of tinkers (or gypsies), traveling people, who scorn houses and move from place to place in brightly painted horse-drawn caravans. They are not unlike the covered wagons of the American Wild West, except that they are made of wood and are far more substantial. The tinker men (they were originally tinsmiths) now make a living by trading in horses, while their women do a modest sideline in fortunetelling.

Tinkers have always had a reputation for being light-fingered and wouldn't think twice about whipping up a fine fat chicken if it chanced to stray onto the road. They have a novel way of cooking a chicken. First they wring its neck to kill it. They neither pluck nor gut the chicken. The feathered bird is plastered over with a thick casing of soft mud. A hole, about a foot deep, is dug in the ground and the mud-encased chicken is put into this. The hole is filled in with earth and a brisk fire is lit on top. The chicken is thus safely hidden from the sharp eyes of inquisitive policemen.

When the fire has died down—about three or four hours later —the chicken is dug up. It is now encased in a hard ball of clay, which is smartly cracked with a hatchet. All the feathers and skin come clean away, to reveal the snow-white breast and the legs of the nicest chicken you ever ate. I know, for I once did it. The feathers give it an unusual flavor and the gut inside keeps the flesh moist.

Tinkers do the same thing with hedgehogs and with the fish they tickle out of the streams.

I mention this only because, in a way, it proves that the more primitive the cooking method the better the result. I heard, only recently, that this same chicken dish is offered by wealthy Chinese to their most honored guests. So now.

Turkey

The small, white-feathered turkeys, with their exuberant bosoms, are enjoying a great vogue today. They are far more economical to carve than the old-fashioned bronze turkeys. But they don't taste like turkey the way their bronze cousins did. They are more like double-breasted chickens.

I won't bother to mention roast turkey, because that is, after all, a classic dish in America, but sometime you might try a boiled turkey. This was a great favorite with my mother, who wouldn't thank you for a roasted bird.

BOILED TURKEY AND CELERY SAUCE

1 8-pound hen turkey	Salt and pepper
2 carrots	1 bunch parsley
2 onions	1 sprig thyme
1 bay leaf	1 ham bone (optional)

Put the turkey and all the other ingredients into a saucepan with enough boiling water to cover. Bring to a boil. Skim. Simmer gently for 1½ hours, or until the legs feel springy under the pressure of your finger and thumb. Turn off the heat and leave the bird to set in the water while you make the sauce (given below).

CELERY SAUCE:

1 large head celery
2 to 3 cups strained turkey
   soup
3 tablespoons butter
3 tablespoons flour

1 cup milk
¼ teaspoon powdered mace
Salt and pepper
½ cup cream

Cut away all the green part of the celery. Cut up the white heart in 1-inch lengths. Boil until tender in the turkey soup. Strain and hold the celery aside, keeping the liquid for the sauce.

Melt the butter. Add the flour. Cook together for 2 minutes. Gradually add the boiling milk while stirring well. Add the hot liquid in which the celery was cooked. Stir to keep smooth. Cook for 10 minutes. Add the cooked celery, seasonings, and, lastly, the cream. Drain the turkey. Pour half the sauce over it and serve the rest separately.

Any turkey that is left over should be returned to the cooking liquid to get quite cold. This will be moist and juicy when you eat it next day.

Turkey bones make wonderful soup.

UNCLE GEORGE'S TURKEY

Uncle George was a doctor and he always had plenty of syringes around. It was he who first taught me how to inject cream into a turkey. He always held that it made the flesh—especially the flesh in the leg—much less dry.

1 turkey
1 medical syringe
½ cup cream

Fill the syringe with cream and inject generously into the legs of the bird and more frugally into the breast. Paint the bird all over with melted butter and roast in the usual way.

This might be a good idea with frozen fowl, which tend to be so dry, though I must honestly admit I never cooked a frozen bird.

Goose and Duck

I much prefer a goose to a turkey. Think of that nice dark flesh and the crackle of crisp skin.

In the country in Ireland the first goose of the season is eaten on Michaelmas Day (September 29). At that time the young birds have not grown to their full size, and, although they are beautifully tender, there is not much flesh on them. A Michaelmas goose, weighing 9 to 10 pounds, would feed no more than 6 to 7 people.

MICHAELMAS GOOSE

1 young goose 8 to 9 pounds	¼ cup water
	Flour to dredge
2 tablespoons goose fat or beef drippings	

POTATO STUFFING (traditional Irish):

2 pounds raw potatoes	½ teaspoon chopped thyme
2 onions	1 leaf of sage, crumbled
The goose liver, chopped	Salt and pepper
1 tablespoon butter	

Boil the potatoes in salted water in their jackets. Peel and mash them while still warm. Lightly fry the onions and liver in butter. Add to the mashed potatoes, together with the herbs and seasonings. Be generous with the pepper, as the stuffing should taste slightly "hot."

Put the stuffing into the belly of the bird and sew up the vent.

Do not overstuff, or the stuffing will swell and burst out in the cooking. Plaster the bird with the drippings and lay on a roasting pan with the water. Bake for approximately 2 hours in a moderate oven (360°). Baste from time to time. In the last half-hour, dredge the breast with a little flour. Baste with hot fat and allow to crisp. *6 servings.*

These Michaelmas geese have not yet run to fat, so they need to be well basted. The stuffing is very nice, I think, because it has a pleasant taste of goose. (How surprising!) You dig it out with a spoon when you are carving the goose.

Applesauce is always served with goose and duck in Ireland.

APPLESAUCE:

3 *cooking apples*	½ *tablespoon* (*or less*)
2 *tablespoons water*	*butter*
1 *tablespoon sugar*	*A little grated orange peel*

Peel and core the apples. Slice thinly and add to the water and sugar. Boil with the lid on till they are soft. Sieve. Return to the saucepan and add the butter and the grated peel. Stir well and reboil. This yields approximately 1 cup of sauce.

CHRISTMAS GOOSE

Christmas goose is a different story altogether. By December the geese are as fat as Victorian matrons. They have spent the whole of the autumn foraging around in the stubble fields in search of fallen corn and barley. And they are as greedy as can be. By Christmas they are barely able to waddle.

1 fat goose 13 to 14 pounds
2 bitter apples

It is not a good idea to stuff a fat goose, as there is too much fat in the flesh and the stuffing would be greasy. Instead, put the ap-

ples, cut in two, inside in the belly. They will help to counteract the fat.

Lay the goose on a grid standing over the roasting pan. Put
into a hot oven (400°) for a half-hour. This will help to crisp
the skin. Reduce the heat to 350° and prick the skin lightly
with a fork from time to time to allow the fat to escape. Do not
damage the flesh. Bake for 2½ to 3 hours. Cooked in this way,
the bird will not be in the least greasy.

By the way, you should always cherish the drippings of a goose.
It is excellent for sprains and is still used by apothecaries as the
basis for all sorts of healing ointments. I had a great-uncle who
used to rub it on his head as a cure for baldness, but I can't
remember whether it was effective or not.

Goose bones are excellent for soup.

Goose liver, floured and fried in butter, is the king of all the
liver tribe.

I once had a cousin in Kerry who, every Christmas, sent a fat
goose to his uncle in England. Inside the goose he concealed a
large bottle of poteen—his uncle's favorite tipple. There was one
unfortunate occasion when the English landlady put the goose
in the oven, not realizing that the illicit spirit was inside it. After
some time there was an unmerciful explosion.

DUCK

> 1 young duck 4 to 5 pounds
> POTATO STUFFING as for Michaelmas goose
> 1 tablespoon goose drippings or beef drippings

Stuff the duck. Lard it with the goose or beef drippings. Put it in
a hot oven (400°) for 20 minutes. Baste it. Lay the duck on its
side so that the legs will cook well. Reduce the heat to 350°.
After another 20 minutes, baste again and turn the duck on his
other leg and leave him so for 10 minutes. Finish baking the

duck on his back so that the breast will get brown. Time 1¼ to 1½ hours. *4–5 servings.*

Duck is nice with mashed potatoes to which the grated rind of an orange has been added.

Game

ROAST WILD DUCK

1 *wild duck*	1 *tablespoon Irish Mist*
1 *onion*	*liqueur*
2 *slices fat bacon*	1 *orange*

Put the onion into the belly of the duck. Tie the slices of bacon over the breast and put the bird into a hot oven (400°) for 20 minutes. Remove the bacon. Add the liqueur, the juice of the orange, and half the grated rind. Baste well. Bake a further 15 minutes. Season and degrease the gravy and serve over the duck.

All these small birds should be baked in small containers. If you put them into a large roasting pan the gravy will dry up. *1 or 2 servings.*

GROUSE

My father was considered the best grouse shot in our parish, and it was not unusual for him to return home on the evening of the Twelfth of August (the opening of the grouse season) with fifteen or twenty brace of birds in the bag. I think a lot of the credit went to Tara, our red setter dog, who was one of the greatest gun dogs in Ireland—or so father thought.

What a to-do there was on the morning of the Twelfth! The whole household was astir by six o'clock. The lunch basket was packed—two roast ducks, a cake of brown bread slit in two and heavily spread with fresh country butter (churned by mother the night before), a bunch of scallions, and a hunk of cheese. Two dozen bottles of Irish stout and a bottle of whiskey were stored in the well of the jaunting car, together with the guns, the lunch, and all the other impedimenta for a day on the heather.

If the morning was wet, my father and my older brother poured a naggin of poteen into their heavy boots to keep out the damp and ward off the cold. By seven o'clock they were on their way, with Tara sitting up in front excitedly wagging his feathered tail, and the pointer, Cormac, barking his head off.

They never returned until nightfall, and we all sat up until the early hours listening to their talk about the birds they shot and the ones that got away, while Tara lay, his head resting on my father's warm, slippered foot, asleep.

Of all birds, surely grouse are the choicest, with their plump breasts and their distinctive flavor.

When cooking game it is important to remember that the flesh should be larded well with bacon or fat pork. They have been running from danger all their lives, poor things, unlike the cosseted domestic birds, and have had little chance to put on condition.

ROAST GROUSE

2 *young grouse*	2 *strips fat pork*
¼ *pound stewing steak*	1 *tablespoon butter*

Divide the steak in two and put a piece into the belly of each bird. This is important, as it will keep the flesh moist. Then tie the fat pork over the breasts and paint the back and legs with

the butter. Put them into a small roasting pan so that they will
fit snugly into it. Cover the pan with a loose-fitting lid, or lay a
piece of aluminum foil over the breasts. Do *not* put foil tightly
over the pan, as this causes the birds to stew rather than roast.
You want to let some air at them, but not too much. Put into
a medium oven (350°) for 40 to 50 minutes. Remove the fat
pork from the breast toward the end of the baking time. If you
like your game rare you would, of course, bake for less time. That
is all a matter of taste.   *4 servings.*

If the birds are old (young birds have smooth legs, while in
the older ones the legs tend to be scaly), they will be tough if
you roast them. You must settle for long, slow cooking in a casserole. But this, too, is very rewarding, because you end up with
the most wonderful game stew and a gravy that will stick to your
ribs.

STEWED GROUSE

2 elderly grouse
2 tablespoons flour
Salt and pepper
2 tablespoons bacon fat
   or butter
2 onions, sliced
2 carrots, sliced

¼ pound mushrooms,
   sliced
1 bay leaf
¼ pound pork sausages
1 tablespoon Irish Mist
   liqueur
1½ cups good stock

Cut the birds into quarters. Toss in seasoned flour and brown
gently in the melted bacon fat. Line the bottom of the casserole
with the sliced onions, carrots, and mushrooms (we always used
wild mushrooms for this) and put the meat resting on them.
Now add the sausages, liqueur, stock, and bay leaf. Season again
and cover with a very tight lid. Cook in a slow oven (320°) for
2 hours. Stir before serving to bring up the rich, thick gravy from
the bottom.   *4–6 servings.*

PHEASANT

I always roast pheasants in exactly the same way as grouse, i.e., a lump of steak in the belly and the breast well larded with fat pork. And I always cook it for 1 hour. Game is nicer eaten at home than in a restaurant, because few people who are dining out will wait long enough for the birds to be cooked at a gentle heat.

When making the gravy for roast pheasant or grouse, make sure to up-end and drain the bird over the roasting pan when you take it out of the oven. Remember, there is all that wonderful juice lying around the steak in the belly. That is what fortifies game gravy and puts it in a class by itself.

In Ireland roast pheasant and grouse come to the table surrounded by a ruffle of game chips. These are a frightful nuisance to make at home. It is much more sensible to go out and buy a few packets of potato chips and warm them in the oven.

Then there are the fried breadcrumbs that were also part of the game ritual in Victorian days. Nobody bothers with them now. The sort of people who can afford to eat game nowadays are all worried about their waistlines and wouldn't be seen dead in the company of breadcrumbs, even unfried.

SNIPE AND WOODCOCK

These are not gutted. They are trussed with their own beaks, buttered well, laid on squares of toast and roasted in a 400° oven. The snipe gets 12 to 15 minutes, while the woodcock takes 20 to 25 minutes. The toast catches the juice from the bird and is served with it.

VENISON

The traditional Irish way of cooking venison is to roll it in a thick paste made from flour and water and cook it on a spit in front of a brisk wood fire. But first, catch your deer. If you have the good fortune to be married to a huntsman (careful he doesn't shoot you, too), I know of no better way to eat this timorous beast, except that nowadays you could compromise by baking your haunch in a moderate (350°) oven until the crust is a nutty brown. Now remove the crust, smother the flesh with boiling butter, and return to the oven to brown faintly.

RABBIT

Until about ten years ago Ireland was overrun with wild rabbits. They became a positive plague in the country, eating the vegetables in the gardens and the crops in the fields. At one time they could be bought in the city shops for twelve cents apiece, while in the country they cost no more than the price of a shotgun cartridge. Then came myxomatosis, a deadly rabbit disease, which all but wiped out the rabbit population. Alas, it also put an end to a valuable source of cheap food. It was always looked upon as the poor man's chicken, and there are many who prize its gamey flesh far above the most delicate fowl. (Not me.)

RABBIT STEW

1 young rabbit	2 white turnips
1 tablespoon vinegar	6 slices of bacon
2 carrots	1 bay leaf
2 onions	1 sprig fresh thyme
2 white stalks celery	1 bunch parsley
2 potatoes	Pepper

Cut the rabbit into 6 or 8 portions. Soak them for 1 hour in a bowl of water to which you have added a tablespoon of vinegar. Wipe rabbit dry and throw away the water. Slice the carrots, onions, and celery, the potatoes and turnips. Lay half the vegetables in the bottom of the casserole. Add the bacon and the jointed rabbit. Put the rest of the chopped vegetables on top. Now add the bay leaf, the thyme, and the bunch of parsley. Season with the pepper but no salt (the bacon provides enough). Pour on sufficient cold water almost to cover the vegetables. Put a tight lid on top of the casserole and cook in a slow oven for 1½ hours, or until the rabbit falls from the bone. Throw away the thyme and parsley. Stir up the stew, so that the potatoes will thicken the juice. Fish out the pieces of rabbit and pile them in the center of a dish, with slices of the bacon around them. Pour the cooking juice over all.

Sometimes the potatoes are omitted and the rabbit and bacon are smothered in a thick PARSLEY SAUCE. *6 servings.*

A WORD ABOUT EGGS

Ubh gan salann, póg gan croimbéal.

(An egg without salt is like a kiss from a beardless man.)

WHAT a wonderful food is the egg. So delicate, so versatile, and so good for you.

In Ireland we give dozens of raw eggs to our race horses and to our greyhounds. That is why they have such shiny coats and such great stamina. We use the lightly beaten white of an egg as a beauty mask for our faces and we wash our hair with the yolk.

Unless it is unavoidable, eggs should not be stored in a refrigerator. A cool larder is the proper place for them. If you must keep them in a refrigerator, you should take them out an hour before you want to use them and leave them standing in a warm kitchen. Eggs that are ice cold will not whip, so they are useless for cakes. The whites will refuse to foam up into a stiff snow, so you cannot make a proper soufflé. The yolks will sulk and give you a cracked mayonnaise.

Oddly enough, *very* fresh eggs behave in exactly the same way. (I am talking now about eggs that have come straight from the nest—a thing that concerns only people who have their own hens.) Ideally, an egg should be twenty-four hours old before it is used in any cooking, except to boil it.

There is no place where a fresh egg shows to such advantage as in the simple dish of bacon and eggs. To do the job properly, the eggs should be dropped on the pan, one at a time, and basted with the fat from the bacon. But, if you have to feed six people all at one sitting, this personal service is not always feasible. You can short-cut the proceedings by dropping all six eggs on the pan (they *must* be fresh eggs), giving them one baste with the bacon fat and then covering the pan with a lid. The yolks will coat over with a film of white—and they will all be cooked together.

We in Ireland tend to think of America in terms of big cities —New York, Boston, Philadelphia, San Francisco—but there are vast tracts of the United States where people live on farms and rear their own chickens. For them I include these notes on how to preserve eggs. This is a regular practice among farmers' wives in Ireland, where eggs are cheap and plentiful in spring and summer but go into the Bull Market in December, when all the Christmas baking has to be thought of.

If you do live in the country and have the generous impulse to send your city relatives a box of fresh eggs from your farm, you should always "hot-butter" them first. You can't imagine what a delectable flavor the butter gives to the egg—and it will keep, in mint condition, for six weeks.

HOT-BUTTERED EGGS

Take the eggs fresh from the nest. Wipe lightly if they are stained, but do not wash. Smear your hands with butter and completely envelop each egg in a thin coating of butter. Store in papier-mâché egg trays with the narrow, pointed end of the egg down. The trays can be stacked one on top of another. These eggs take on the subtle flavor of the butter. Boiled or fried, they are superb.

TO PRESERVE EGGS WITH LARD

½ cup lard
¼ cup powdered borax

Mix the lard and borax to a smooth paste. (The lard preserves the eggs and the borax preserves the lard.) For this method the eggs must be at least twelve hours out of the nest—otherwise they will take up the taste of the lard—but not more than twenty-four hours old. Smear your hands with the mixture and completely grease the eggs. Put in papier-mâché egg containers (with the pointed end of the eggs down). Stack the containers, one on top of another, and store in a cool, dry place.

The eggs need not all be done at once. You need only preserve your surplus eggs from day to day. There is sufficient in the lard and borax mixture given above to coat twenty-five dozen eggs.

But it is important (don't ask me why) that the eggs are stacked with the narrow, pointed end down.

Eggs preserved in this way will keep perfectly for six months.

Sterile eggs are considered by some to be better for preserving than the eggs of hens that have been respectably married. But I doubt if it makes any difference. We always had great success with our preserved eggs, though we had the most magnificent cocks running around the farm.

BACON AND EGG TART

3 slices bacon	Salt and pepper
1 onion	Short-crust pastry (given
3 eggs	below)
2 cups milk	

Fry the bacon. Remove it from the pan and cut into thin strips. Chop the onion and fry in the bacon fat. Beat the eggs. Add the milk and seasoning. Add the bacon strips and fried onion. Pour into an 8-inch pan lined with short-crust pastry and bake in a moderate oven (350°) until brown and firm.

SHORT-CRUST PASTRY:

2 cups flour	½ teaspoon salt
1 cup butter	Ice water

Crumb the flour and butter together with your fingers. Add the salt and sufficient ice water to make a very stiff dough. Chill for a half-hour. Grease an 8-inch pan. Roll out the pastry and line the pan with this. Pour the egg mixture into this and bake as above.

For a pleasant alternative add 2 tablespoons of grated cheese to the egg mixture. Then you can omit the fried bacon. Eat the tart hot or cold. *6 servings.*

HAM AND POACHED EGG

4 fresh eggs
1 cup chopped ham
1 cup cheese sauce (given below)

Lightly poach the eggs. Drain them. Put them in a pie dish and cover with the chopped ham. Mask them with the cheese sauce and brown under the broiler. This is an excellent way of using up the end of a piece of ham.

CHEESE SAUCE:

2 tablespoons butter
2 tablespoons flour
1 cup milk (approx.)
½ cup grated Parmesan
   or any other sharp
   cooking cheese

A pinch of powdered
   mace or nutmeg
Pepper

Melt the butter. Add the flour and stir well. Cook for 2 minutes. Add hot milk gradually. Stir to prevent lumps. Cook for 5 to 10 minutes to take away the flour taste. Add cheese, spice, and pepper. Taste for saltiness, as you never know with cheese. Salt if necessary. Pour over the eggs and ham and brown them under the broiler. *2–4 servings.*

WICKLOW PANCAKE (traditional)

4 eggs
2 cups milk
2 cups white breadcrumbs
6 scallions, chopped
1 tablespoon chopped
   parsley

½ teaspoon chopped thyme
1 tablespoon butter
Salt and pepper

Beat the eggs. Add milk, breadcrumbs, scallions, and herbs. Season. Melt the butter in a heavy pan. When hot, pour in the mixture and let it set over a slow heat. When firm on top, turn, and brown on the other side. This pancake is quite thick. Cut in 4 sections and serve with a pat of butter on top. *4 servings.*

EGGS MIMOSA

6 eggs
Salt and white pepper
2 tablespoons mayonnaise

Hard-boil the eggs for 10 minutes. Crack the shells and peel when cold. (The shells should always be cracked immediately the eggs come out of the pot. This allows the sulphur to escape and prevents that dark border from forming around the yolks.) Cut the eggs in two across the waistline. Remove the yolks. Cut a small section off the rounded top of each half (can you follow this?) so they will have a flat base to rest on. Fill the upturned cups of eggwhite with mayonnaise. Sieve the egg yolks and season. Pile on top of the mayonnaise. Nice with assorted cold meats.

I know this doesn't sound like much, but it is really rather nice. When you cut through the egg you come upon the soft, runny center. Like the pleasant surprise of biting into a liqueur sweet. *3 or 6 servings.*

ROASTED EGGS

One of the great treats of my childhood was to roast eggs in the ashes under the fire in the sitting room. The eggs were pierced once with a pin, to let the sulphur fumes escape. They were then left in the warm ashes for about a half-hour. When we raked them out they were quite hard. They had a most unusual taste. I had quite forgotten about them until now.

I am going to skip all the exotic and wonderful things you can do with eggs. Although soufflés and omelets and such like are commonplace in Irish homes today, they really do not belong in a native Irish cook book.

But I'll tell you an interesting thing I discovered about a savory soufflé like, say, a cheese soufflé. It is all the better for being put into a cold oven before switching on the heat. Contrary to popular belief, a soufflé should be baked in a moderate oven (350°) for 40 to 45 minutes. It should rise gradually, like a careful government servant, consolidating its position on the way up.

Did you know that mayonnaise gets its name from an Irishman, General MacMahon? It was originally called *Mahonnaise* by the general's French chef, who invented it.

VEGETABLES

Is maith na fataí nuair bhíos an bláth bán orthu.

(When the blossom grows white the potatoes are good.)

EXCEPT in the city centers, almost everyone in Ireland has a plot of ground—big or small—where the basic vegetables are grown for the family. And no self-respecting plot owner would neglect to grow a few drills of early potatoes, so that he can enjoy the pleasure of pushing in his spade and digging out his own fresh and succulent tubers.

This reminds me of a story I heard from Barbara Bel Geddes, the famous American actress, when she was spending a summer in the West of Ireland with her family. Every day, around noon, Michael (the gardener) left a basket of vegetables and a basket of freshly dug potatoes at the kitchen door. These were cooked for the family lunch.

The children took a great interest in Michael's activities, and one morning the eldest rushed into the house, shouting: "I've just seen Michael getting the potatoes. They came out of the ground . . . like, like uranium. I always thought they grew on trees."

Potatoes play an essential part in the diet of the Irish. We eat them every day as a vegetable. They are used in some of the distinctive Irish breads. In former times they were often used as a leaven in baking.

In order to get the true flavor of young potatoes they should be freshly dug out of the ground (some hope, in the city!). Then the skin will peel off by rubbing it with your thumb.

BOILED NEW POTATOES

1 pound new potatoes of uniform size	*Boiling water*
	1 sprig mint
1 teaspoon salt	*Chopped parsley*

Skin the potatoes by scrubbing with a soft brush (or by rubbing with your thumb, if they are really fresh). Salt the boiling water. Add the mint and potatoes. Boil them until tender (about 12 to 15 minutes). You can always test them with a fork. Drain well, so that there is no water in the bottom of the pot. Discard the mint. Cover the pot with a clean, folded cloth (to absorb the steam) and put it back on a gentle heat so that the potatoes inside dry off. It is very important that potatoes should get a chance to dry, otherwise they will be soapy. Toss lightly in butter and serve with a sprinkle of chopped parsley and chopped mint on top.

P.S. New potatoes are always put into *boiling* water, while old potatoes are started off in cold water.

As the potato season advances, you may find that certain strains of potatoes tend to burst their skins and disintegrate in the pot. There is one certain cure for this. Boil the potatoes in sea water. But where would you get sea water if you live in a city?

BAKED JACKET POTATOES

> 6 large old potatoes
> ½ tablespoon butter
> ½ teaspoon coarse salt

Prick the potatoes here and there with a fork—this releases some of the starch. Mix the salt with the butter and rub over the potatoes. Bake in a hot oven for 1 hour. Test with a fork to ensure that they are soft all through. You can eat the skin, too.

ROAST POTATOES

> 6 medium potatoes
> 1 tablespoon flour
> Salt and pepper

Peel the potatoes and leave to steep in cold water for 1 hour. Dry well. Toss in the seasoned flour and put in the pan beside the meat when you are cooking a roast of beef. Baste whenever you baste the joint. When cooked, they should be crisp and brown outside, while the inside is light and floury.

CHAMP (for children)

> 1½ pounds potatoes
> 6 scallions
> Water
> 1½ cups milk
>
> Pepper
> 1 teaspoon salt
> 4 pats butter

Peel the potatoes and steep in cold water for 1 hour. Cover the potatoes with cold salted water and boil until tender. Drain well and dry off by laying a folded cloth on top and returning the pot to a gentle heat for a few minutes. Now mash the potatoes. Chop the scallions very finely, using the green tops as well as the young bulbs. Put them into a bowl and scald by pouring boiling water over them. (This keeps the tops bright green.) Drain them well. Add them to the milk and bring to a boil. Pour the milk and scallions into the mashed potatoes. Add pepper and taste for salt. Beat until light and fluffy.

Champ is served on individual soup plates in little mounds. A crater is scooped out at the peak and a pat of butter dropped into the center.

This is a traditional Irish dish. I can well remember eating it when I was a child. The soft potato was scooped up with a spoon from the outer edges. It was then dipped in the well of butter at the center. How lovely it tasted then.   *4–6 servings.*

COLCANNON

1½ pounds potatoes	1 tablespoon butter
1½ cups milk	1 tablespoon chopped
6 scallions	parsley
1½ cups boiled green	Pepper and salt
cabbage or curly kale	

Boil the potatoes and mash as for CHAMP (given above). Add the boiling milk and scalded, chopped scallions and beat until fluffy. Toss the cooked cabbage, finely chopped, gently in the melted butter. Add to the potatoes, together with the parsley, and fold well. Season generously with pepper and taste for salt.

This is very Irish and far nicer than it sounds. In some districts the cabbage is omitted.   *6–8 servings.*

Traditionally, colcannon is always served at Hallow's Eve. A miniature thimble and horseshoe, a button, a silver sixpence (dime), and a wedding ring are each wrapped in white paper and dropped into the mixture. These forecast the fortunes of the finders. If your portion contains the ring, you will marry and live happily ever after. The silver sixpence denotes wealth, the horseshoe good fortune, the thimble a spinster, and the button a bachelor.

POTATO FLOUNCES

6 *medium-sized potatoes*   *Salt and pepper*
2 *large onions*
½ *tablespoon butter*
1 *cup rich milk or ½*
   milk and ½ evaporated
   milk

Peel the potatoes and slice very thinly. Leave them to soak in cold water for 1 hour. Skin the onions and slice in thin rings. Drain the potatoes and dry in a cloth. Grease a pie dish with butter. Put in alternate layers of potato and onion. Season as you go along, and put a knob of butter here and there through the layers. Pour in the milk and finish with a layer of potatoes that have been arranged like the flounces on a petticoat. Press down well. Smear with the rest of the butter. Bake in a hot oven (400°) until soft all the way through. *4–6 servings.*

CABBAGE

Cabbage is frowned upon by many epicures. This is particularly true of people who are forced to eat a lot of their food in restaurants. Cabbage is an abomination to them. And I don't blame them, because, unless cabbage is freshly picked, cooked, and served immediately, it can be dreadful. There is no vegetable that spoils quicker.

But if you eat cabbage (as in the simple dish of bacon and cabbage) in an Irish home, it is a different matter altogether.

When cooking cabbage, it is a good idea to put a peeled onion in with the cabbage. This helps to counteract the rather unattractive smell.

There are three main types of cabbage grown in Ireland, and each has its own devotees.

First, there are young spring greens—these are at their best when the plants are just beginning to heart. When allowed to grow to maturity they can be so tough that it is impossible to cook them without adding a pinch of baking soda, to soften the fibers.

Next, we have the drumhead, or white, cabbage. This plant is round and firm. It is not as interesting as "spring greens," but it is excellent eaten raw in a cabbage salad or boiled in water that has been flavored with a ham bone.

Lastly, we have the cabbage with the crimped or serrated leaves. This is a winter cabbage and stands up well to frost. It is not as flavorsome as either of the other strains.

SPRING GREEN CABBAGE

2 heads of young green cabbage	1 onion
	Black pepper
Salt	½ tablespoon butter

Trim away the coarse leaves. Cut out the tough ribs that run along the center of the leaves. Wash well in salted water. Boil rapidly, with the lid off, in a pan of salted water to which a peeled onion has been added. If the cabbage is fresh, it will be cooked in 10 to 15 minutes. Drain well in a colander by pressing a plate on top. Pepper well and glaze with the melting butter. This should be eaten immediately.

In parts of Ireland this cabbage is finely chopped after it is drained. I think this takes away from its appearance. *4 servings.*

BOILED WHITE CABBAGE (drumhead)

1 cabbage, approximately 2 pounds	1 onion
Boiling water	Pepper
1 ham bone or 3 cups ham stock	Grated nutmeg
	2 teaspoons butter

Cut the cabbage in quarters and remove the tough inner stalk. Shred the cabbage across the grain in inch strips. Wash in cold salted water. Drain. Plunge it into a pan of fast-boiling water, to which you have added a ham bone, or 3 cups of the water in which ham or bacon has been boiled. This addition should salt the water enough (if you have neither the bone nor the ham water, you must, of course, use salt in the cooking water). Add the skinned onion and cook for 5 to 10 minutes, or until the cabbage is tender but still has body.

Drain very well. Dust with pepper and grated nutmeg and serve with melting butter on top. *6 servings.*

P.S. A half tablespoon of bacon drippings added to the water will improve the flavor if you have not got a ham bone to hand.

CREAMED CABBAGE

1 white cabbage, approximately 2 pounds	1 tablespoon flour
Boiling water	Salt and pepper
1½ tablespoons butter	½ grated nutmeg
	1 cup evaporated milk

Quarter the cabbage and cut away the tough stalk. Plunge the quartered cabbage into a pan of fast-boiling salted water. Cook for 5 minutes (with the lid off). Drain well and refresh under the cold faucet. Cut the quarters, across the grain, in half-inch strips.

Melt the butter in a saucepan and add the shredded cabbage. Stir it around in the melted butter. Sprinkle in the flour, salt and pepper, and the nutmeg, and stir well with a wooden spoon, so that the flour is well mixed. Add the evaporated milk and bring to a boil. Put the lid on the saucepan and cook very gently for 30 minutes. You may stir from time to time, in case it might burn. This is very good. *6 servings.*

CABBAGE SALAD

1 *small white cabbage*	*Salt and pepper*
1 *clove garlic, crushed*	2 *tablespoons olive oil*
(optional)	*with 1 tablespoon lemon*
½ *tablespoon chopped*	*juice (or 3 tablespoons*
chives	*mayonnaise)*
½ *tablespoon chopped*	
parsley	

Quarter the cabbage and remove the tough stalk. Shred the quarters across the grain in very thin slivers. Soak in ice-cold salted water for a half-hour to crisp. Dry in a tea cloth. Rub the bowl with the crushed clove of garlic. Add shredded cabbage, chives, parsley, and seasoning. Toss in the oil and lemon juice (or use the mayonnaise). *6 servings.*

ONIONS

It is a wonder to me that onions have been so neglected as an independent vegetable. We put them into stews, all right, and we wouldn't think of making a soup without them, but so few people will give them the dignity of serving them all by themselves. I can't imagine why. They are so bland and delicate when cooked—and they are so good for you. Many wise old people in Ireland eat a boiled onion last thing at night to ward off insomnia. And you will never have any trouble with your digestive tract if you treat yourself to a boiled or baked onion every day.

I think it is because they are so cheap, and so readily available throughout the year, that onions have lost their popularity. There is no greater snob than the epicure.

BOILED ONIONS

4 large onions	Butter
Boiling water	Black pepper
Salt	

Skin the onions—this can be done under cold water if they tend to make you weep. (Or you could wear a pair of goggles!) Put the onions into a pot of boiling salted water and cook gently until they are tender. You can test them by sticking a skewer down the center. They generally take about 1 hour. Lift them out of the water and drain well. Serve with a pat of butter on top of each onion and plenty of black pepper. The onion water can be tipped into soup. 6 servings.

BAKED ONIONS

4 large onions
Aluminum foil

Put the onions (unskinned) on an ovenproof plate and cover loosely with aluminum foil. The covering is only to prevent the onion juice from spurting all over the oven, but you must have some air around the onions. Bake in a hot oven for about 1 hour.

When I am cooking a roast of beef I always bake potatoes and onions in the same oven. They are all cooked together—and so little trouble.

Onions cooked in this way are superb. All the pungent sulphur comes out of them and you are left with the soft hearts that are as delicate as oysters. *4 servings.*

*   *   *

BRUSSELS SPROUTS

Here is another vegetable that is often scorned. And I don't wonder. Brussels sprouts, as served in restaurants, are always diabolical. They have probably been cooked for hours and have taken on a dirty yellow color. Avoid them. Indeed, the sprouts that are grown by market gardeners are no great shakes either. They have all been blown up by artificial fertilizers and are sometimes as big as apples. Dreadful.

The true Brussels sprouts are tight little buds, no bigger than walnuts, and they can be very nice if you cook them at home. But the odd thing about them is that, unlike cabbage, you get tired of them if you eat them often.

1 pound small sprouts	*1 teaspoon butter*
1 teaspoon salt	*Black pepper*
Boiling water	

Trim the sprouts and discard the loose outside leaves. Soak them in cold salted water for a half-hour. Put them in a pan of boiling salted water and cook until tender but still firm. If the sprouts are really fresh and small, they will be cooked in 10 to 15 minutes. Drain them well, glaze with butter, sprinkle with black pepper, and serve at once.

It is most important not to overcook sprouts. They should retain a definite "bite" under your teeth. *3–4 servings.*

CAULIFLOWER

Cauliflower is acceptable only with certain meats. With roast beef, yes, or with roast lamb, or with a brown stew. But it is dreary with chicken or veal (too white), and quite unthinkable with any fish.

When choosing cauliflowers always pick the small heads, no bigger than a grapefruit. They have more flavor and are far easier to handle in the cooking. Large cauliflowers are better split up in quarters before cooking.

2 small cauliflowers	1 tablespoon crushed,
Boiling water	crisped rinds of bacon
Salt	(given below)
½ cup milk	

Soak the cauliflowers for 1 hour in heavily salted cold water. Drain. Plunge them into a pan of boiling water, to which you have added a teaspoon of salt and the milk. The milk keeps the flowers white. Cook them until tender but still firm. (It is important that the flowers should not become mushy.) Drain on a tea cloth. Dust over with the bacon. Put under the broiler for a moment. The bacon rinds give a nice crunch to the dish. *4 servings.*

CRUSHED BACON RINDS:

Save the rinds from several slices of bacon. Put them in a roasting pan in a hot oven and cook them until they are completely crisp. Drain well and crush roughly with a rolling pin. Store in an airtight jar.

BUTTERED CARROTS

When cooking carrots, *never* cut them across the grain into those dowdy circles. They look far prettier if they are cut into 2-inch lengths and are then quartered along the grain of growth. In Ireland buttered carrots are traditionally served with IRISH STEW. They add a nice touch of color to the white of the potatoes.

4 good carrots	½ teaspoon sugar
Boiling salted water	Pepper
½ tablespoon butter	2 teaspoons chopped chives

Peel the carrots and cut as explained above. Plunge them into boiling salted water and cook until tender. Drain well. Add the butter and sugar to the saucepan with the carrots. Shake well until the carrots are fully buttered. Season them with pepper and serve with the chopped chives scattered on top. *4 servings.*

BABY CARROTS

Baby carrots, which should be no bigger than your thumb, are cooked whole and unskinned.

12 small young carrots	Salt and pepper
½ cup water or chicken	½ teaspoon sugar
stock	Chopped parsley
½ tablespoon butter	

Top and tail the carrots and put into a saucepan with all the ingredients except the parsley. Press a piece of wax paper or aluminum foil well down on the vegetables and put the lid on the saucepan. Boil rapidly for 10 minutes. Remove the paper or foil. Shake the saucepan over the heat until the carrots are nicely glazed. Pepper them well and serve with chopped parsley on top. *3 servings.*

P.S. A few very small onions cooked with the carrots will help the flavor.

PARSNIPS AND TURNIPS

Parsnips and turnips were used extensively in rural Ireland to give variety in the winter, when green vegetables were scarce. With the advent of frozen vegetables they have fallen from favor and are now looked upon as old-fashioned.

I think the time will come when they will regain their former popularity. I know I have rediscovered parsnips again after ignoring them for twenty years. Who would have thought that Victorian bric-a-brac, which was considered so hideous no more than ten years ago, would now become collectors' pieces? And so it may happen with parsnips and turnips.

TOASTED PARSNIPS

2 or 3 parsnips, 1 pound each	½ teaspoon sugar
½ tablespoon butter	Pepper

Peel the parsnips. Cut them in 2-inch lengths across the grain. Cut the lengths down into quarters or eighths. Boil them in salted water until tender—20 to 25 minutes. Drain them thoroughly and put a folded cloth on top of the saucepan to enable the parsnips to dry off. Melt the butter in the frying pan. Toss in the cooked parsnips, sprinkled with the sugar. Pepper well and brown on all sides. Or you could put the buttered parsnips under the broiler and toast. Nice with roast beef. *6 servings.*

MASHED TURNIPS

Swede turnips (the yellow turnips, or rutabaga) are a regular stand-by for the Irish housewife with a large family. They are cheap and they are a favorite with children. The sweet, peppery taste of these modest roots, eaten in an Irish home (never in a restaurant) is a pleasing experience. The yellow turnip may be substituted.

1 yellow turnip, 1½ to
    2 pounds
Boiling salted water
1 cup freshly mashed
    potatoes

½ tablespoon butter
Salt and pepper

Peel the turnip. Cut it into 1-inch slices. Drop into a pan of boiling salted water. When tender, drain very thoroughly and return the pot to the heat to allow the turnips to dry off. Mash to a fine pulp. Add the dry mashed potatoes, the butter, and plenty of pepper and heat all together.

This dish should be very peppery. *6 servings.*

PEAS

In Ireland the first of the season's peas are always eaten with young lamb. Ideally, peas should be picked, podded, and cooked all within a half-hour. If they have been picked fresh from the plant, they will be cooked within 5 to 7 minutes. Peas that have been lying around in shops will take longer.

IRISH PEAS

3 pounds peas in the pod   1 sprig mint
1 teaspoon sugar   2 teaspoons butter
Boiling salted water   Salt and pepper

Pod the peas. Put into a pan of boiling salted water with the mint and sugar. Boil gently until tender—about 5 to 7 minutes. Strain and finish off by shaking lightly in the butter and seasoning. If you start off with fresh young peas this is a classic dish. The peas are bright green in color and very delicate and sweet to eat. *6 servings.*

FROZEN PEAS

This is a trick I discovered myself about frozen peas. Instead of following the directions on the package, try the following:

½ tablespoon butter
1 package frozen peas
Salt and pepper

Put the butter in a saucepan with the frozen peas. Put a tight lid on top and put the saucepan on a gentle heat. Shake the saucepan from time to time so that the peas will heat through. Do *not* use water, do *not* add sugar, and do *not* cook the peas. Just warm them right through by agitating in the saucepan over the heat. When they are all nicely heated, remove the lid to let any unwanted moisture escape. Season and serve with a little butter melting on top.

If you cook frozen peas like this, they do retain their taste and bite, and the color is excellent. *4–6 servings.*

MUSHROOMS

Field mushrooms are, of course, the kings of the whole tribe. They have such a fragrant smell and are so beautiful to behold, with their white caps and their pleated pink gills. How often have my sisters and I gone hunting for mushrooms in the early mornings in August and September, when the dew was still on the grass. We would carry them home in a milk can and cook them for breakfast.

The larger mushrooms were fried in the pan with the breakfast bacon, but the perfect cups that had just opened enough to reveal their pink petticoats were given more delicate treatment. First the stalks were carefully removed so as not to damage the cups. The cups were then placed, skin down, on the top of the hot range. A pinch of salt was dropped into the center of each, and, when the center had filled with its own juice, the mushrooms were cooked. There you have mushrooms at their simplest—and best.

MUSHROOMS IN BUTTER

When you buy cultivated mushrooms, you should never skin them. The best part of the flavor is right there. It is enough to rub them with your thumb, or with a soft cloth, to remove sand or grime.

I had always been disappointed with the texture and flavor of cultivated mushrooms until I evolved this simple trick:

¼ pound small mushrooms
Salt and pepper
1½ tablespoons butter

Rub the skins of the mushrooms lightly with a clean cloth. (This may not be necessary if the mushrooms have been well harvested.) Trim stalks level with the lip of the mushrooms. Slice each mushroom in two or three segments, or leave them whole if they are very small. Melt the butter in a saucepan. Put the mushrooms into the butter. Cover with a tight lid and shake over a low heat. Do *not* cook the mushrooms. All you want to do is *heat* them through. Season before serving.

Mushrooms done in this way do not become tough and black. But don't add salt until you have finished heating them. The salt draws out the juice. *2–4 servings.*

*   *   *

PARSLEY

Traditionally, parsley is sown on Good Friday. If it grows in abundance, it is said to indicate that the woman of the house wears the trousers.

Since parsley is used to adorn, it is a matter of pride to an Irish cook that *her* parsley should be a bright emerald green and very finely chopped. In order to achieve this standard of perfection, here is what you must do:

1 generous bunch of young parsley, freshly picked from the garden if possible.

Chop the parsley very finely, discarding the stalks and all tired leaves. Put the chopped parsley into a square of muslin, or the corner of a clean tea cloth, and gather the cloth around it. Run the cold faucet on your bag of parsley while you squeeze it with your finger and thumb. Now squeeze dry in your fist. Toss it out onto a plate and, if the parsley is fresh and young, it is a true emerald green.

FRIED PARSLEY

16 sprigs of parsley
Deep fat for frying

The sprigs should be young and fresh and with a little stalk attached. They should be bone dry, otherwise they will make an unmerciful splash in the hot fat.

Put them in a wire basket and lower gently into the smoking fat. They make a frightful noise when they are cooking. When the spluttering stops—it is all over in a minute—the parsley is crisp and a bright green. Nice as a garnish for fish but very bothersome unless you are using the deep-fat frying for something else.

GARLIC

Garlic grows wild in parts of Connemara and the Aran Islands. The cows are very fond of it, and sometimes you will get a very faint trace of garlic in their milk. It is elusive, and not in the slightest degree unpleasant.

My parents put great faith in garlic (and whiskey) as a panacea for all ills. On our kitchen dresser there always stood a bottle of Irish whiskey with two or three dozen peeled cloves of garlic inside it. Temperatures, tonsils, stomach-ache were all treated with this homemade medicine. The nauseating brew was poured down the patient's throat. It was enough to put anyone off whiskey for life.

The animals got their share of it too. Chickens with the croup, turkeys with blackhead, cows with the murrain, horses with the strangles were all treated with the same medicine. It occupied about the same place in our household as penicillin does in modern therapeutics.

*   *   *

All the more sophisticated vegetables are now readily available in Ireland, but I have deliberately left them out because they are not indigenous here. I could tell you nothing about their cooking that you don't already know—except perhaps this trick about cucumber:

CUCUMBER SALAD

½ cucumber
¼ teaspoon salt
1 teaspoon oil

2 teaspoons vinegar
Pepper

Skin the cucumber and slice in very thin rings. Put in a soup plate. Sprinkle the salt on top. Put the bottom of another soup plate resting on the cucumber. Put a 2-pound weight on top and leave for 1 to 2 hours. Pour off the liquid that is drawn out of the cucumber and discard. Dress the cucumber with the oil, vinegar, and pepper.

This treatment makes the cucumber very easy to digest. *3 or 4 servings.*

BREAD AND CAKES

Ná mól an t-arán go mbruithtear é.

(Don't praise the bread until it is baked.)

Bread

ONE of the great traditions of Irish cooking is the excellence of our homemade bread. The Irish soda bread and the brown bread that are still baked daily in every farmhouse in Ireland are considered to be among the best kinds of bread in the world.

And they are so easy to make. No sponging and proving as for yeast bread. The leaven used is bread soda in conjunction with buttermilk, and the bread is in the oven within 5 minutes of opening a package of flour.

I only wish I could recapture for you the sweet, crusty smell of a cake of bread fresh out of the oven, or the taste of a farl of oaten cake, running with butter.

Since bread is the very staff of life, it always amazes me that sophisticated adults who would scorn anything less than *la grande cuisine* will tolerate the poor quality of commercial bread all over the world today.

The great variety of Irish breads owes its existence to the traditional eating habits of our people. Throughout the country-side breakfast is an important and leisurely meal that usually includes porridge, tea, and eggs in some form. Dinner is eaten in the middle of the day. In rural Ireland, farmers working in the fields return home at one o'clock with healthy appetites. They need a hearty meal. In the smaller towns shopkeepers and office workers are within walking distance of their homes and can return in time to eat with their wives and children.

At six o'clock comes "tea." This may consist of boiled eggs, the ubiquitous bacon and eggs, or cold meats and salad. But it is always accompanied by a variety of home-baked breads, buns, and cakes. A good housewife would scorn to offer a visitor anything less than three distinct types of her own bread, an assortment of scones, and two or three cakes for good measure—all freshly baked for the occasion.

It is mainly for this six-o'clock tea that an Irishwoman extends herself at baking. And it is because of this tradition that so many varieties of bread have been evolved in Ireland.

Buttermilk plays an important part in our bread. To describe for you how buttermilk is made, I must take you back again to my childhood, because homemade buttermilk is fast disappearing, even in Ireland.

Cows, as you no doubt know, are milked twice a day—in the early morning and in the evening. In our house, when the fresh milk came in from the byre, it was customary to strain off two or three jugfuls (sufficient for the household requirements) and set them aside. The rest of the milk was strained into large earthenware crocks where it was left, undisturbed, in the dairy until it soured and thickened. In the summertime this took no more than two or three days (in thundery weather it would turn overnight). In winter it took much longer.

When the milk was thick and ripe, it was tipped into a revolving barrel churn that was rotated with a handle at the side. The churn was turned round and round on its axis until some instinct told one that it was time to unscrew the lid and scald the milk. A kettle of boiling water was poured into the churn, the lid reclamped, and, moments later, the butter had separated from the milk and formed itself into solid lumps in the liquid. Cold spring water was now added. The butter was collected in a wide wooden bowl, washed in running water, salted, and shaped into oblongs, each weighing about 1 pound. But some was kept aside and put into little wooden molds. When the pats of butter no bigger than a dollar—were pressed out, they had the imprints of the shamrock, the rose, or the thistle on them.

If I live to be a hundred, I shall never forget the sweet-salt taste of fresh country butter.

But I am digressing. The liquid left in the churn, after the butter is removed, is the buttermilk. Fresh buttermilk is sharp and tart and very refreshing to drink. It is far above water, or beer, as a thirst quencher. I have known men who would drive ten miles in the pony-and-trap to a house that had freshly churned buttermilk if they were suffering the aftereffects of a wedding or a wake. There is no swifter or better cure for a hangover.

Except in farmhouses, fresh buttermilk is rare enough in Ireland today. The bulk of the milk now goes direct to the creameries, and we bake our bread with sweet milk or with milk that is soured at home.

TO SOUR MILK FOR IRISH SODA BREAD

4 cups whole milk
2 teaspoons lemon juice

Tip the milk into an earthenware jug. Add the lemon juice and stir. Leave in a warm place—near the stove or in an airing cupboard—until the milk is thick. The milk should be ready in 24 to 36 hours. If pasteurized milk is left *too* long to sour, it tends to go rotten.

With your 4 cups of sour milk you are now in the bread-baking business. As you use up the soured milk, fresh milk is added to the jug and allowed to ferment. In this way you have an unending supply. But it is important to remember that every third day the milk must be transferred to another jug that has been scalded with boiling water and refreshed under the cold faucet. By doing this you prevent putrefaction.

If all this business about souring milk frightens you, don't worry too much. I myself sour the milk for baking in a jug over the mantel shelf in the kitchen, but as often as not I make the bread with ordinary whole milk. The results have always been satisfactory.

Now a word about the ingredients. To reach its classic heights, IRISH SODA BREAD demands the following:

1. Flour that is freshly milled
2. Buttermilk that is freshly churned
3. Baking soda that is finely smoothed
4. A brisk turf fire
5. A bastable oven

This is, of course, a counsel of perfection. The flour is now bought in the supermarket and nobody questions its age. Buttermilk is not what it was. With rural electrification the old-fashioned turf fire has disappeared from the kitchen, and the bastable ovens have gone into folk museums.

This bastable oven, known in parts of the country as the pot oven, was an all-purpose iron pot with a lid which was used for baking and roasting. (I have described it in the recipe for IRISH STEW.) Whether it was the thickness of the iron pot or the soft heat that glowing turf generates I honestly do not know, but this produced bread at its best.

Another bread-baking utensil extensively used in Ireland was the griddle. This was a flat, round iron plate about 16 inches in diameter. It was placed on a trivet at the side of the open fire with a nest of glowing turf sods underneath. A flattened cake of soda bread, no more than 1 inch thick, was put on the griddle. The cake was either cut into four farls (old Irish word for *quarter*) or was marked with a cross through the center so that it would more easily break into farls when cooked. Halfway through the cooking the bread was turned and left to get brown on the other side. All this took place on the open hearth, and it was easy for the woman of the house to keep an eye on it as she went about her work.

Then there were the "hardening stands." These were made of cast iron, perhaps in the shape of a horseshoe or a gate. They stood on the hearth, facing the fire, and thin OATCAKES leaned against them to dry and harden in the heat of the fire. These were a type of unleavened biscuit made from pinhead oatmeal. Eaten hot from the "stand" and running with butter, they were one of the great treats of my childhood.

This bread could be stored and would keep indefinitely without spoiling. Many an Irish emigrant on his way to America in the last century carried a box of oaten bread to sustain him on the journey.

I mention these simple methods of cooking since it is because of them that our distinctive breads evolved. Fuel, in the form of turf, was cheap and plentiful, so the extravagant open-hearth fire was used for baking bread instead of the more thrifty brick ovens employed in the rest of Europe. Bread that could be swiftly put together and baked in the pot oven or on the griddle, in the afternoon when the house was quiet and the pot oven was free, resulted in daily breads both simple to make and unique in flavor.

Yeast bread has become vulgarized with commercialization. In Ireland the fashionable restaurants follow the pattern of international cooking, but they all have a baking woman in the stillroom who makes Irish brown bread to delight the customers. Nobody would think of eating smoked salmon, or Galway oysters, without a few slivers of brown bread on the side.

IRISH SODA BREAD

1 tablespoon butter or
  margarine
4 cups white flour
1 teaspoon salt

1 teaspoon baking soda
1 cup buttermilk or 1 cup
  sweet milk

Rub the butter into the flour. Add the salt and soda, mix all well together by running the dry ingredients through your fingers. Add the buttermilk (or the sweet milk) and stir into a soft dough with a wooden spoon. With your floured hands knead lightly into a ball and turn out onto a lightly floured baking sheet. Flatten the dough into a circle 1½ inches thick with the palm of your hand. Make a cross in the center with a floured knife. Bake at 425° for 30 to 35 minutes.

There is an excellent Irish Soda Bread Mix on the American market.

HOME-BAKED BROWN BREAD

The important ingredient in brown bread is the whole-meal flour, also known as whole-wheat flour. This is the whole wheat kernel crushed to a rough powder. Ideally, it should be crushed between millstones to give it the texture of coarse sand. This is known as stone-ground meal. The bran is not removed (as is the case with white flour) in the milling. The presence of the bran and the rough crushing of the grain produce a bread that is pleasantly gritty under the teeth. It is excellent for the digestive tract.

I am not sure whether you can get stone-ground whole meal in America. I have many American friends who used to bring back home with them a suitcase packed with our whole meal. (I had taught them how to make the brown bread.) But I find it hard to believe that a country that can command the treasures of the world is without this modest item.

The making of bread, as distinct from the more formalized cakes, is something that comes with experience. It is a matter of touch, and instinct and practice. You could make bread every day for a week, and each day it would be slightly different. And no two Irishwomen agree on the exact quantities of this-and-that that go into the finished product. In every house the bread tastes different, but everywhere it is good.

BROWN BREAD (1)

4 cups stone-ground
   whole-wheat flour
2 cups white flour
1½ teaspoons salt

1½ teaspoons baking soda
2 cups buttermilk, sour
   milk, or sweet milk

Mix the whole-wheat flour thoroughly with the white flour, salt, and soda. Make a well in the center and gradually mix in the liquid. Stir with a wooden spoon. You may need less, or more, liquid—a lot depends on the absorbent quality of the flour. The dough should be soft but manageable. Knead the dough into a ball in the mixing bowl with your floured hands. Put it on a lightly floured baking sheet and with the palm of your hand flatten out in a circle that is 1½ inches thick. With a knife dipped in flour make a cross through the center of the bread so that it will easily break in quarters when it is baked.

Bake at 425° for 25 minutes, reduce the heat to 350°, and bake a further 15 minutes.

If the crust seems too hard, wrap the baked cake in a damp tea cloth and leave standing upright until it is cool.

The bread should not be cut until it has set—about 6 hours after it comes out of the oven.

BROWN BREAD (2)

The same ingredients as for BROWN BREAD (1) with:

  1½ tablespoons butter
  ½ tablespoon sugar

Rub the butter into the flours. Add all the other dry ingredients and continue as for the above recipe. The butter makes the bread nice and brittle.

*   *   *

GRIDDLE BREAD

This is made in exactly the same way as IRISH SODA BREAD except that the dough is flattened to no more than 1 inch. It is then cut in quarters and placed on a hot, floured griddle and cooked on top of the stove on a low heat. After 15 to 20 minutes, when the underside is lightly brown, the farls, or quarters, are turned and cooked on the other side for the same length of time.

YELLOW MEAL BREAD

The principal ingredient in this bread is maize flour, known in Ireland as "Golden Drop."

2 cups white flour
2 cups good quality corn meal
1 teaspoon baking soda

1 teaspoon salt
1 cup buttermilk or sweet milk*

Mix all the dry ingredients well together with your fingers. Add the milk. Form the dough into a round ball with your floured hands. Put it on a floured baking sheet and flatten into a circle 1½ inches thick. Make a cross through the center and bake at 425° for approximately 35 minutes.

TREACLE BREAD

Molasses is known as "treacle" in Ireland.

2 tablespoons molasses
1 cup milk (approx.)
1½ tablespoons sugar
A good pinch of ground ginger

4 cups flour
½ teaspoon salt
1 teaspoon cream of tartar
1 teaspoon baking soda

Heat the molasses until it liquifies and add to the milk. Mix all the dry ingredients together. Moisten with the liquid to make a soft dough. Shape into a round cake with your floured hands— about 1½ inches thick. Cut in quarters. Put on a floured baking sheet and bake at 400° for approximately 40 minutes.

Very good for children.

* If sweet milk is used add a teaspoon of cream of tartar to the dry ingredients.

POTATO CAKES (1)

2 tablespoons butter
1 cup flour
½ teaspoon baking powder

½ teaspoon salt
3 cups freshly mashed
  potatoes

Rub the butter into the flour. Add the baking powder and salt
and mix well. Add the potatoes and bind all together with your
hand. Roll out to quarter-inch thickness on a well-floured board
with a well-floured rolling pin. Cut in squares or stamp out with
a cutter. Bake on an ungreased griddle until brown on both
sides. Serve hot with running butter. *Yields 12 cakes.*

Cold potato cakes are often fried with the breakfast bacon.

POTATO CAKES (2)

1 tablespoon flour
½ teaspoon salt
2 cups freshly mashed
  potatoes

2 teaspoons bacon drippings
  for the griddle

Sprinkle the salted flour over the potatoes and knead lightly together. Roll out on a floured board to quarter-inch thickness.
Cut in quarters or stamp out into rounds. Put on a greased
griddle and cook on an even heat until both sides are well
browned. When cooked, butter generously and eat at once.
Yields 6–8 cakes.

BOXTY

Boxty is seldom made in Ireland now, but I include it here because it will bring back nostalgic memories to many people who remember eating it in their youth.

2 *large raw potatoes*	1 *teaspoon baking soda*
2 *cups mashed potatoes*	½ *cup flour* (*approx.*)
1 *teaspoon salt*	

Grate the raw potatoes. Add to the mashed potatoes and salt. Mix the soda with the flour and add to the potatoes. Roll out on a floured board to a circle of a half-inch thickness. Cut in 4 quarters and put on an ungreased griddle. Cook on a gentle heat for 30 to 40 minutes, turning the bread at half time. The farls, or quarters, should be well browned on both sides. *4 servings.*

Sometimes a teaspoon of caraway seeds was added to the dough.

OATCAKES (Old-fashioned)

2 *cups roughly crushed oats*	*Extra crushed oats for*
½ *teaspoon salt*	*rolling*
½ *cup hot water*	

Mix the oats and salt. Add the hot water and bind together with a spoon. (At this stage the dough is very soft.) Leave for 1 hour to steep. Turn out onto a baking board that is generously scattered with crushed oats. Dust more oats over the dough and roll out as thinly as possible. If the dough tends to stick, add more and more oats during the rolling. Cut into 4 quarters. Put on an ungreased baking sheet and bake at 350° (turning from time to time to prevent steaming) for roughly 30 minutes, or until the cakes are crisp and lightly browned. Or cook on the griddle until the farls, or quarters, curl, then transfer to the oven to crisp. *4 servings.*

This is the traditional oaten cake that was also baked on the "stands" in front of the turf fire. It was eaten hot, running with country butter.

It is impossible to reproduce the true flavor of this bread nowadays. So much depends on the fact that the oats should be fresh from the mill.

OATCAKES (Modern)

2 cups roughly crushed oats
½ teaspoon salt
¼ teaspoon baking soda
½ cup butter or margarine

⅓ cup hot water
Plenty of crushed oats for
the baking board

Mix together the oats, salt, and soda. Melt the butter and add to the water. Add enough liquid to the oats to make a soft dough. (You don't want the dough to be firm at this stage.) Scatter plenty of crushed oats on the baking board. Turn out the soft dough onto the board. Scatter more oats on top. Press out with your knuckles, keeping the dough dry, top and bottom, by the addition of more oats. Now roll out as thinly as possible, scattering more oats on top and rubbing them in with the palm of your hand. Cut in squares and bake on a gentle griddle over the stove until it dries and curls. Toast in a moderate oven (320°) to cook the top and crisp the oatcakes. *Yields 12 cakes.*

These cakes can be eaten hot, with plenty of butter, or stored in an airtight container.

They are excellent for young children, as they must be chewed well, so they strengthen the jaws and teeth.

TEA SCONES

½ cup butter
4 cups flour
2 teaspoons baking powder
½ teaspoon salt

¼ cup sugar
1 egg
1 cup milk (approx.)

Rub the butter into the flour, add the baking powder, salt, and sugar, and mix well. Beat the egg and add to the milk. Mix the liquid into the dry ingredients to make a manageable dough—neither too firm nor too slack. Turn onto a floured board, roll to 1 inch thick, and cut into rounds with a pastry cutter. Arrange on a lightly floured baking sheet and bake at 420° until risen and brown, approximately 15 minutes. *Yields 18 scones.*

BROWN TEA SCONES

2 cups flour
2 cups whole-wheat flour
½ teaspoon salt
½ cup butter

2 tablespoons sugar
2 teaspoons baking powder
1 egg
¾ cup milk (approx.)

Mix the flour and whole-wheat flour together with salt. Rub in the butter. Add the sugar and baking powder. Mix well. Beat the egg and add to the milk. Moisten dry ingredients with the liquid while stirring with a wooden spoon. Shape into a ball with your floured hands. Turn onto a board that is well dusted with wheaten meal and roll to the thickness of 1 inch. Cut in small rounds with a cutter. Put on a lightly floured baking sheet and bake at 425° for approximately 20 minutes. *Yields 18 scones.*

PANCAKES

Shrove Tuesday is the traditional day in Ireland for making vast quantities of pancakes for serving at teatime.

In order to make successful pancakes the first essential is a heavy iron frying pan, as you need a strong heat to cook the pancakes quickly.

1 cup sifted all-purpose flour	1 egg yolk
A pinch of salt	1¼ cups milk
1 egg	¾ tablespoon melted butter

Sift the flour and salt together. Beat the egg and egg yolk with the milk and stir some of it gradually into the flour until the batter is the consistency of thick cream. Add the butter and beat with a rotary beater to incorporate plenty of air. Add the remainder of the egg and milk. Beat again and allow to stand for 2 hours. This resting of the batter helps to digest the flour.

Heat the pan well. Grease it lightly with butter. Pour a little of the batter (about 2 tablespoons) on the pan and agitate the pan so that the batter coats it thinly. Cook until brown on one side. Turn it over and cook it on the other side. To keep pancakes warm, put them on a plate over a pan of boiling water, loosely covered with a cloth.

To serve, lightly butter the pancakes, dust with fine sugar, and sprinkle with lemon juice. Roll up into cylindrical shapes. *Yields 12 pancakes.*

PORRIDGE

Since porridge is made from grain, I am tacking it onto the end of the chapter of bread. I can't think of anyplace else to put it. All children in Ireland are nurtured on porridge, and you should just *see* how well they look.

(1) PORRIDGE:

> 2½ *cups water*
> ½ *cup rolled oats*
> ¼ *teaspoon salt*

Bring the salted water to a boil. Sprinkle in the rolled oats, stirring all the time and keeping the liquid on a fast boil to avoid lumps. Reduce the heat and let the porridge simmer for 25 minutes, stirring from time to time. Serve hot with rich cold milk. *6 servings.*

Most young children like this with a teaspoon of honey or maple syrup on top.

(2) ALTERNATIVE METHOD OF COOKING:

Put the 2½ cups of boiling salted water in the top of a double boiler. Sprinkle a half cup of rolled oats into the salted water. Stir well to avoid lumps. Cook for 40 minutes, stirring from time to time.

For Babies: Strain 2 tablespoons of the cooked porridge through a fine strainer and give to babies of 4 months or over. This jelly is known as flummery. In olden times it was flavored with lemon and sugar and served as a pudding. It was the ancestor of modern jellies.

Porridge for breakfast is very good for the whole digestive tract and very soothing for the stomach. Nothing better for warding off Madison Avenue ulcers.

Cakes

Perhaps the most distinctive Irish cake is the barmbrack. It is the only surviving example of the use of yeast in our traditional cooking.

In the early days of the Abbey Theatre, Lady Gregory would always arrive from Coole Park, her home in County Galway, with a barmbrack in her holdall. It was her custom to preside at tea in the Green Room surrounded by writers and actors; W. B. Yeats, J. M. Synge, Lennox Robinson, Sean O'Casey, and a supporting cast that included Barry Fitzgerald, Arthur Shields, Sara Allgood, Maire O'Neill and a host of others who later went on to make international reputations in the theater. This barmbrack became affectionately known as the Gort cake.

A barmbrack is a light, yeasty, fruitcake that is always sliced and spread with butter before eating. At Hallow's Eve (October 31) the barmbrack is baked with a wedding ring wrapped in paper and mixed into the dough. If your slice of brack contains the wedding ring, you will be engaged before the year is out.

BARMBRACK

4 cups flour	2 eggs, well beaten
½ nutmeg, grated	1½ cups sultana raisins
A pinch of salt	1 cup currants
2 tablespoons butter	⅓ cup chopped candied
1 cake of yeast (¾ ounce)	fruit peel
2 tablespoons sugar	1¼ cups milk

Sift flour, nutmeg, and salt together. Rub butter into the flour. Cream the yeast in a cup with a teaspoon of the sugar. Add the rest of the sugar to the flour mixture and mix well. Lightly warm the milk to body temperature. Add to the liquid yeast and most of the well-beaten eggs. Beat the liquid well into the dry ingredients until the batter is stiff but elastic. Fold in the raisins, currants, and fruit peel. Turn into a buttered 8-inch cake pan so that the dough only half fills the pan. Cover with a cloth and leave to rise in a warm place (the airing cupboard or near the stove) until the dough has doubled its size. This takes roughly 1 hour. Brush the top with a little beaten egg to give a glaze. Bake at 400° for approximately 1 hour, or until a skewer, pushed into the center of the cake, comes out clean.

SPONGECAKE

4 eggs   1¼ cups sifted cake flour
¾ cup sugar   Jam
Boiling water   Whipped cream
Grated rind of ½ lemon

Beat the eggs and the sugar in a bowl over a pot of boiling water until thick and creamy. Remove from the heat and beat for 5 minutes longer. Add the grated lemon rind and fold in the well-sifted flour.

Grease 2 shallow 7-inch pans. Line the bottom of each with wax paper. Divide the mixture evenly between them. Bake at 350° until the cakes shrink from the sides of the pans—about 20 minutes.

Cool them a little before turning out onto cooling racks. When they are quite cold, remove the paper and join both cakes together, after having filled the center with jam and whipped cream.

SPONGE LOZENGES

Drop some of the spongecake mixture in teaspoons on lightly floured baking sheets. Leave 1 inch between each blob, as the mixture will spread. Bake at 350° for 5 to 6 minutes.

Cool and join in pairs with whipped cream.

BUTTER SPONGECAKE

This is a nice cake with a close texture.

¾ cup butter or margarine	1½ cups sifted cake flour
½ cup sugar	1 teaspoon baking powder
3 eggs	Jam or whipped cream

Beat the butter and sugar until creamy and white. Add the eggs, one at a time, together with a dust of flour to keep them from curdling. Make sure to beat well after each egg. Fold in the sifted flour and baking powder. Divide the mixture between 2 well-oiled shallow 7-inch pans. Bake at 400° for 25 minutes. Reduce heat for the last 10 minutes.

Let the cake shrink for 5 minutes in the pans before turning out on the cooling rack. When it is cold, spread the bottom half with jam or whipped cream (or both) and place the top half over it.

SEEDCAKE

This was a great favorite when I was young. It was offered to lady visitors with a glass of port if they called in the morning or the afternoon. To drink the wine on its own would not have been considered respectable.

1 cup butter
1 cup sugar
4 eggs
2½ cups sifted cake flour
½ teaspoon baking powder
1¼ teaspoons caraway
   seeds

2 tablespoons Irish
   whiskey
Extra caraway seeds for
   dusting on top

Cream the butter and the sugar together until white and fluffy. Add the eggs, one at a time, with a dust of the flour. Beat well after the addition of each egg. Sift the flour with the baking powder and fold gently into the egg mixture with the caraway seeds. Add the whiskey and pour the mixture into an 8-inch cake pan that has been lined with wax paper. Scatter some caraway seeds on top. Bake at 375° for 1 hour. Reduce the heat toward the end of the baking time.

P.S. If you don't like caraway seeds, you can add 1½ cups sultana raisins instead.

CHERRY CAKE

1 cup butter
1 cup sugar
5 eggs
A little grated lemon rind
3½ cups sifted cake flour

½ teaspoon baking powder
1½ cups glacé cherries
3 tablespoons ground
   almonds

Cream the butter and sugar together until white. Add the eggs, one at a time, and beat well between each egg, remembering to dust a little flour over each egg as you break it into the bowl. Add the lemon rind. Sift the flour with the baking powder and fold gently into the mixture. Toss the cherries in the ground almonds and stir into the mixture. Bake in an 8-inch cake pan that has been lined with wax paper at 350° for approximately 2 hours.

DUBLIN CAKE

This is very Irish. A substantial fruitcake for a family.

3½ cups sifted all-purpose
    flour
1 cup brown sugar
1 cup butter or margarine
½ teaspoon baking soda
4 eggs
½ teaspoon salt
2 to 3 tablespoons Irish
    stout

1½ cups raisins
1½ cups sultana raisins
1½ cups currants
½ cup candied fruit peel
Grated rind of 1 lemon
½ teaspoon mixed spice

Cream the butter and sugar and add the lemon rind. Add the eggs, one at a time with a teaspoon of the flour, and beat well between each egg. Sift flour with salt, soda and spice. Fold into egg mixture. Moisten with 2 to 3 tablespoons of the stout. Stir in fruit. Put into an oiled pan (9-inch) that is lined with wax paper. Bake at 350° for 2½ to 3 hours. Reduce the heat in the last hour. When cold this is sliced and buttered like bread.

IRISH WHISKEY CAKE

1 lemon or 1 orange
2 tablespoons Irish whiskey
1¼ cups sultana raisins
¾ cup butter
¾ cup sugar

3 eggs
2½ cups sifted cake flour
A pinch of salt
¾ teaspoon baking powder

With a sharp knife peel the rind off the lemon (or orange). Soak the rind in the whiskey for a few hours to draw out the flavor. Discard the rind and soak the sultanas in the whiskey. Cream

the butter and sugar. Add the eggs, one at a time, with a teaspoon of flour, and beat well after adding each egg and flour.
Sift flour, salt, and baking powder together and fold into the egg
mixture. Lastly fold in the sultanas and whiskey. Put into an
oiled 7-inch cake pan that is lined with wax paper. Bake at
350° for 1¼ to 1½ hours. Reduce heat toward the end of baking time. Eat while fresh.

CHRISTMAS CAKE

When I first published this recipe in the *Irish Times* ten years
ago, I got thousands of letters from people, all over the world,
who had made the cake with great success. There is a whole
street in Rome where the inhabitants make it every Christmas
(an Irishwoman living there who is married to an Italian passed
on the recipe), and I have had charming letters from housewives in such faraway places as Hong Kong and Trinidad.

This is an old recipe of my mother's. I don't deserve any
credit for it.

½ cup glacé cherries	1½ cups chopped walnuts
1 cup seedless raisins	1½ cups butter
1½ cups sultana raisins	1½ cups sugar
1 cup currants	7 eggs
½ cup mixed candied fruit peel	4 cups sifted cake flour
2 tablespoons finely chopped angelica	1 teaspoon salt

Some hours before making the cake the following preparations
are necessary. Halve the cherries. Put all the fruits and the nuts
into a casserole. Mix them well together with your hands, so
that the different species are well distributed. Cover loosely with
paper or aluminum foil and put into a warm oven (240°) until

the fruit is well heated through. You might toss the fruit over once or twice to allow the heat to penetrate. This heating makes the fruit sticky and prevents it from falling to the bottom of the cake. It also plumps the fruit and makes it juicier. Never roll fruit in flour—this toughens the fruit and makes the cake dry. And don't wash the fruit—you are removing the natural sugar.

When the fruit is well heated through and is sticky, take it out of the oven and let it get *quite cold*. Warm fruit added to a cake mixture would melt its way down to the bottom before the mixture had set in the oven.

Now, back to the cake.

Cream the butter and sugar together until white and fluffy. Add the eggs, one at a time, with a teaspoon of flour for each egg. This prevents the eggs from curdling the mixture. Beat well between each egg.

Sift the flour with the salt and fold into the egg mixture. Lastly, fold in the fruit and nuts, which you have separated by running your fingers through them.

Put the mixture into a high 10-inch cake pan that has been oiled and well lined, sides and bottom, with two thicknesses of strong paper. The mixture, which you flatten in the pan, should not come up to more than 2 inches from the top of the pan. Trim the lining paper level with the top of the pan and rest an inverted tin plate or a lid over the top of the pan.

Put the cake in a slow oven (300°). Reduce to 280° after 1 hour. Remove the lid after 2 hours and continue the baking for another 3 hours, about 6 hours in all.

If you think the cake is baking too fast, keep gradually reducing the heat. This cake should be golden rather than brown on top. Do not remove from the pan until cold.

The secret of success with this cake is the plumping of the fruit, the covering of the cake for the first 2 hours, and the slow baking.

ALMOND SHORTBREAD

1 cup butter	1⅓ cups sifted cake flour
½ cup sugar	¾ cup blanched almonds
1 egg	1½ tablespoons extra sugar

Cream the butter and sugar. Add the egg and beat till fluffy. Fold in the flour. Grease a baking sheet, 10 by 14 inches, that has low sides. Spread the mixture evenly and thinly on the sheet with a knife. Halve the blanched almonds and mix with the extra sugar. Scatter this loosely over the paste. Bake at 300° until pale gold. Cut across into squares when it comes out of the oven, but leave in the sheet to get cold. *Yields 18 cookies.*

This is a very nice biscuity confection and keeps perfectly in an airtight container. It is probably the nearest thing we have to the American cooky.

SIMPLE MERINGUES

2 egg whites	¾ teaspoon baking powder
¾ cup sugar	1 cup heavy cream

Beat the egg whites to a peak. Continue to beat while gradually adding the sugar. Mix the baking powder with the last tablespoon of the sugar and beat well into the meringue mixture. Put out in teaspoonfuls on ungreased baking sheets, leaving an inch between each meringue, and bake at 250° for 1¼ hours. Reduce heat if necessary. Meringues are prettier if they are a faint beige color rather than pure white.

To serve, whip the cream (no sugar) and put the meringues together in pairs with the cream between. Leave to stand for a half-hour before serving. *Yields 12–15 meringues.*

PUDDINGS AND PIES

I AM afraid the Irish are no match for the Americans when it comes to puddings. Stewed fruit and custard or fresh fruit tarts were the "old reliables" of my youth. Ice cream now replaces the old-fashioned egg custard.

The IRISH COFFEE PUDDING is delectable, though it is both troublesome and extravagant. The STRAWBERRY FLAN is a great favorite with us, probably because fresh strawberries have such a short season, so we don't get a chance to tire of it. The PLUM PUDDING (CHRISTMAS PUDDING) is alarming in its proportions and in the inventory of ingredients. Unless you are married to an Irish husband, I would think twice before undertaking it. At least you can't say I didn't warn you.

IRISH COFFEE PUDDING

6 eggs
¾ cup sugar
1 cup water with 1½
  tablespoons instant coffee,
  or 1 cup very strong
  black coffee
2½ tablespoons powdered
  gelatin

⅓ cup Irish whiskey or
  Irish Mist liqueur
1¼ cups heavy cream
2 tablespoons crushed
  walnuts

Separate the yolks from the whites of eggs. In a bowl cream the yolks with the sugar. Blend the instant coffee with the water (or use strong black coffee). Heat it but do not boil. Completely dissolve the gelatin in the hot coffee and add all to the yolks and sugar. Beat well and put the bowl over a pan of boiling water. Continue beating until mixture begins to thicken. Add the whiskey or liqueur and beat until mixture is thick and creamy. Remove from heat and, when the bowl has cooled a little, put over cracked ice and continue to stir. When the mixture is on the point of setting, whip the cream and fold it in. Lastly fold in the well-beaten egg whites.

Pour into a 7-inch soufflé case that has a collar of strong wax paper tied around it. The paper should come up 3 inches above the top of the soufflé case. Oil a jam jar or a bottle and press it down into the center of the pudding. Leave to set. Remove the paper collar by easing around the circumference with a knife dipped in hot water. Remove the jar (or bottle) and fill the center with:

1 cup heavy cream, whipped
2 tablespoons chopped walnuts

Decorate the exposed sides of the pudding with crushed walnuts that you press on with the palm of your hand.

This is a lot of work but is very nice for a party. *10–12 servings.*

CARRAGEEN PEPPERMINT CREAM

Carrageen moss is an edible seaweed that is found all along the coast of the West of Ireland. It is picked by the fishermen and left to bleach in the sun. It is very easy to digest and is thought to be excellent for complaints of the stomach and chest. I fancy you could buy it in shops that deal in health foods.

1 handful of carrageen moss	*3½ tablespoons sugar*
4 cups milk	*6 drops peppermint oil*
A pinch of salt	*Green vegetable coloring*

Soak the carrageen in cold water for 15 minutes until soft. Rinse well. Boil it with the milk and salt until the liquid is thick and creamy. Add the sugar, peppermint oil, and coloring. Strain to remove carrageen and discard. Leave to set. Serve with cream and chocolate sauce. *4–6 servings.*

CHOCOLATE SAUCE:

3 ounces unsweetened chocolate	*1¼ cups water*
½ cup sugar	*¼ teaspoon vanilla extract*
½ teaspoon instant coffee	*1½ teaspoons cornstarch*

Put the chocolate, sugar, coffee, and water into a saucepan. Boil and stir gently until melted. Simmer for 5 minutes. Add the vanilla and cornstarch, blended with a little water. Boil the mixture again to cook the cornstarch. Serve hot or cold. *Yields 1½ cups.*

VISITORS' TRIFLE

Our family trifle was usually a hotchpotch of anything that was left over from the day before—stale spongecake, the heel end of a jelly, the last of a can of fruit. The whole thing was smothered in a whiskey-flavored egg custard and topped with whipped cream.

But that was not considered party fare, which went like this:

1 stale spongecake
4 tablespoons raspberry jam
⅓ cup Irish whiskey
⅔ cup sherry
2 cups egg custard (given below)

2 egg whites
1 cup heavy cream
½ tablespoon sugar
½ cup almonds, blanched and split

Split the spongecake into 4 layers. Spread the layers generously with the jam and restack. Put them in a glass dish. Mix the whiskey and sherry and pour over the layered cake. Cover with a plate and leave to soak for an hour.

FOR THE CUSTARD:

1 egg
2 egg yolks

1 tablespoon sugar
2 cups milk

Beat the egg and egg yolks together with the sugar. Scald the milk and pour over the eggs while beating. Cook the custard over a pan of hot water until it thickens to a cream. Pour it over the cake while hot. Leave to get cold.

Beat the 2 egg whites to a peak. Whip the heavy cream with a half tablespoon of sugar. Fold the whites into the beaten cream and pile over the trifle. Decorate with the blanched and split almonds, which are spiked into the cream.   *8 servings.*

APPLE TART

This is sometimes called apple cake. It is made on an aluminum plate or on a discarded dinner plate of fine delft. It is not so nice when baked on a plate of glass ovenware, as the material is too thick to let the heat through to the pastry.

1½ cups butter or   *A little ice water*
  margarine (cold)   *4 large cooking apples*
3 cups flour   *3 tablespoons sugar*
A pinch of salt   *6 cloves*

Rub the shortening into the salted flour. Add enough ice water to make a very stiff dough. Chill for 1 hour. Cut off a little more than a third of the pastry. Roll out into a circle that will well cover a 10-inch plate. Dampen the plate by rubbing a wet cloth over it. Put the pastry on the plate and press well down. Peel and core the apples and slice directly onto the pastry. Add the sugar and cloves.

Roll out the rest of the pastry into a circle that is 1 inch larger all around than the plate. Dampen the outer edge of the pastry on the plate with water. (You must leave about a half inch all around that is not covered by the apple.) Lay the second circle of pastry on top of the apples and press well down around the edges, so that the top pastry is stuck to the damp edge. Make 2 small cuts in the center with the point of a knife to allow steam to escape. Trim around with a knife. Bake in a hot oven (400°) until the pastry is golden. Reduce heat to 300° until apples are soft when you test with a skewer. Dust with fine sugar before serving. *8 servings.*

This tart can be made with all the fresh fruits—rhubarb, gooseberries, raspberries, and blackberries—as they come into full season.

APPLE FLUFF

2 eggs
4 cooking apples
2 tablespoons water

2 tablespoons sugar
2 additional tablespoons
  sugar

Separate the yolks from the whites of the eggs. Peel, core, and slice the apples and add to the water and sugar. Cook them until very soft. Sieve the apples and add the beaten egg yolks. Put into a pie dish and top with a meringue made from the egg whites and additional sugar. Bake at 400° until meringue is well colored.

STRAWBERRY FLAN

1 pastry shell (given below)
3 tablespoons red-currant
  jelly

1 cup heavy cream
1 pound fresh strawberries
½ tablespoon water

FOR THE PASTRY SHELL:

½ cup butter (cold)
2 cups flour

1 egg
⅓ cup extra fine sugar

To make the pastry, rub the butter into the flour. Bind together with the beaten egg. Put the sugar on a board and knead the dough in this. Roll out the sugared pastry and line a greased 8-inch pan with it, making sure that it comes up the sides of the pan. Trim. Lay wax paper over the pastry and tuck in at the sides. Scatter split peas or rice on the paper (to keep the shape of the shell) and bake at 350° till pastry has set. Discard the paper and peas (or rice) and dry out the pastry shell in the oven.

When it is cold, spread a thin coat of red-currant jelly on the bottom of the shell. Beat the heavy cream and spread on top of the jelly. Arrange the strawberries on top and glaze with the remainder of the red-currant jelly, which has been dissolved with a little water over gentle heat. Leave to set before serving. 6 *servings*.

This pastry is crisp and biscuity, and you must use butter to get the best effect. This flan can be made in the same way with any fresh fruits: pineapple, peaches, raspberries, etc. It is not so interesting with canned fruit, as you lose the contrast of the tart fruit with the sweet jam.

LEMON PUDDING

2 *eggs*	3 *tablespoons sifted flour*
1½ *tablespoons butter*	2 *cups milk*
½ *cup sugar*	*Sugar for dusting*
Grated rind and juice of	
1 *lemon*	

Separate the egg yolks from the whites. Cream the butter and sugar, add the yolks, the grated rind and juice of the lemon, and the flour. Beat well and gradually add the milk. Fold in the stiffly beaten egg whites. Pour the mixture into a greased pie dish and stand the dish in a bigger dish with about an inch of water in it. Bake at 350° until risen and brown—about 35 to 40 minutes. Dust with sugar before serving. Eat while hot.

This makes a nice pudding with a spongy top, while the bottom is like a creamy lemon custard. *4–5 servings*.

BAKED CUSTARD

2 eggs
2 egg yolks
2 tablespoons sugar

2½ cups milk
1 fresh bay leaf
1 teaspoon butter

Beat the eggs and egg yolks with the sugar. Scald the milk and pour on the egg mixture while beating. Add the bay leaf. Pour into a buttered dish. Dot here and there with the butter. Stand the dish in a larger dish containing 1 inch of water and bake at 350° until firm in the center. Remove bay leaf before serving. This is a favorite dish in Ireland with stewed fresh fruit and cream. *4–6 servings.*

BAKED TOFFEE CUSTARD

Make liquid custard as in previous recipe, leaving out the bay leaf. Pour into individual fireproof dishes and bake in a pan of water until set. Sprinkle a teaspoon of brown sugar on top of each custard and put under a gentle broiler until the sugar has melted and begins to bubble. When it is cold, serve. The sugar will have formed a crisp toffee coating on top. Nice to break into. *4–5 servings.*

COFFEE CUSTARD

Same as BAKED CUSTARD except that you leave out the bay leaf and add ¾ tablespoon instant coffee to the egg mixture. Bake as above. Serve with cream, hot or cold. *4–6 servings.*

PLUM PUDDING (CHRISTMAS PUDDING)

½ cup flour
1½ cups breadcrumbs
1 cup brown sugar
¼ cup finely chopped suet
½ teaspoon salt
½ nutmeg, grated
½ teaspoon mixed spices
¼ teaspoon ginger
¾ cup seedless raisins

¾ cup currants
¾ cup sultana raisins
½ cup candied fruit peel
1 cup chopped almonds
1 apple, peeled and grated
Grated rind and juice of a
  lemon
3 eggs
½ cup stout

Mix the flour with the breadcrumbs, sugar, suet, salt, and spices. Add fruit, peel, nuts, apple, and lemon rind. Beat the eggs and add to the stout and lemon juice. Pour over the dry ingredients and mix thoroughly. You want a soft consistency. Moisten with more stout if too dry.

Pour into greased 6-inch bowls and cover with wax paper, then with floured pudding cloths, and secure them well at the sides. Boil them in a large pot, with the water coming three-quarters way up the sides of the bowls, for 5 to 6 hours. Add more water when necessary. Makes 2 puddings.

When they are cooked, take off the wet cloths and cover the bowls with dry cloths. When cold, store in a refrigerator. When you want them, boil them again for 2 to 3 hours and serve with BRANDY BUTTER (given below). *12 servings.*

BRANDY BUTTER:

½ cup butter
1 cup sifted confectioners' sugar
3 tablespoons brandy or Irish whiskey

Cream the butter until white. Add the sugar and beat well. Gradually add the brandy or whiskey, taking care that the mixture does not curdle. Pile it in a dish and chill till hard.

By tradition, plum pudding is brought to the table on Christmas Day flaming with lighted whiskey or brandy. With spirits so much underproof nowadays, it is a wise precaution to sprinkle some granulated sugar over the pudding after you have poured on a quarter cup of warmed spirits. This should keep the flame alight. In my childhood we always used a good splash of poteen and we had a flame that would singe the rafters.

I always think plum pudding is a frightful trouble with all those hours of boiling. But you daren't set an Irishman down to his Christmas dinner without it.

MINCE PIES (Traditional at Christmas)

MINCEMEAT:

1 large apple	1 cup sugar
2 cups raisins	¼ teaspoon salt
2 cups currants	¼ teaspoon cinnamon
1 cup sultana raisins	¼ teaspoon allspice
½ cup candied fruit peel	¼ teaspoon powdered cloves
½ cup almonds	½ cup melted butter
1 orange	¼ cup Irish whiskey
1 lemon	

Core the apple but do not peel. Mince apple, raisins, currants, sultanas, peel and almonds at the coarse setting of the mincer. Grate the rind off the orange and lemon and squeeze out the juice. Mix the grated rinds with the sugar, salt, and spices. Add the melted butter and spiced sugar to the minced fruit, together with the juice of the lemon and orange and the whiskey. Mix thoroughly with your hands. Store in airtight jars until needed.

PIECRUST:

2 cups butter (cold)	A pinch of salt
4 cups flour	Ice water

Rub the butter into the salted flour. Bind to a stiff dough with a little ice water. Chill for 1 hour. Roll out the pastry very thinly. Cut in rounds with a pastry cutter. Ease the rounds into greased patty pans. Put a good teaspoon (or more) of mincemeat in the center of each round and cover with another round of pastry. Pinch the sides together so that the top hat won't come off in the cooking. Stick the point of the knife twice into the top of each pie to let the steam escape. Bake at 400° until the pastry is colored. The pies are eaten hot, with a light dusting of confectioners' sugar. *Yields 12 small pies.*

BEVERAGES

Is deacair amhrán a rádh gan gloine.

(It's hard to sing with an empty glass.)

THE heading of this chapter reminds me of Oscar Wilde's remark that we are separated from America by the barrier of a common language. In Ireland the word "beverage" applies only to those warm bedtime drinks beloved of insomniacs and to a wide range of nonalcoholic concoctions, including lemonade and Coca-Cola. Everything else is "drink."

Whiskey, which takes its name from the Gaelic *uisgebeatha*, water of life, is the classic Irish drink. They've been making it here since Homer was a boy, and its fame is as old as Methuselah. Four hundred years ago, Richard Stanihurst, a visiting historian and scribe, recognized its remarkable virtues:

It sloweth age; it strengtheneth youth; it helpeth digestion; it cutteth fleume; it abandoneth melancholie; it relisheth the harte; it lighteneth the mynd; it quickeneth the spirites; it cureth the hydropsie; it puffeth away ventrositie . . . and trulie it is a soveraign liquor if it be orderlie taken.

There may be the rare occasion when it is not "orderlie taken," but its enlivening properties are still unimpaired. In Ireland we drink our whiskey neat, or with plain water, but never with ice. Heavens, we need it to warm us.

Stout—a black, yeasty ale with a creamy foam on top—is by far the most popular Irish drink. It was first produced in 1759 by Arthur Guinness, a member of the family that still controls the vast brewing concern, now exporting to all parts of the world. The name Guinness is a synonym for stout in any Irish pub.

This noble brew is often recommended by doctors—in Africa, where large quantities are consumed, it is regarded as an aphrodisiac!

A popular Irish tipple in days gone by was poteen—an illicit spirit produced in homemade stills in remote parts of the country. It was made from fermented grain, by the same process used in distilling whiskey. Carefully handled, and left to mature in sherry casks, it was considered an excellent drink. It had the added advantage of evading excise duty.

But this undercover activity has virtually ceased, and it is almost impossible to buy a bottle of poteen in Ireland today. Many expert poteen makers, disturbed by the attentions of the police, carried their know-how to America and made fortunes during the Prohibition era.

Drinking with friends is a ritual as well as a pleasure among the Irish, and the toast *"Sláinte 'gus Saol agat"* (Health and long life to you) is the usual compliment to the company.

Here is a traditional toast with a fine poetic ring about it:

Sláinte 'gus Saol agat,	Health and long life to you,
Talamh gan Chíos agat,	Land without rent to you,
Bean ar do mhian agat,	The woman of your choice to you,
Leanbh gach bliain agat,	A child every year to you,
Saol fada agus bás in nÉirinn.	A long life, and may your bones rest in Ireland.

IRISH COFFEE (1)

1½ teaspoons sugar
Hot, strong black coffee
1 jigger Irish whiskey

1 tablespoon whipped cream

Heat a stemmed whiskey goblet. Add the sugar and enough of the hot coffee to dissolve the sugar. Stir well. Add the Irish whiskey and fill the glass to within an inch of the brim with more very hot black coffee. Float the cream on top. Do not mix the cream through the coffee. The hot, whiskey-laced coffee is sipped through the velvety cream. *1 serving.*

IRISH COFFEE (2)

1 teaspoon sugar
Hot, strong black coffee

1 jigger Irish whiskey
1 tablespoon double cream

Proceed as for IRISH COFFEE (1) until the goblet is filled with the spiritous coffee to within an inch of the brim. Gently pour the double cream onto a teaspoon that is held over the coffee. The cream spilling over should float on top of the coffee. But this won't work unless the cream is rich and chilled. *1 serving.*

IRISH WHISKEY PUNCH

1½ teaspoons brown sugar	*3 cloves*
Boiling water	*1 slice lemon*
1 jigger Irish whiskey	

Heat a stemmed goblet. Add the sugar and dissolve in a little of the boiling water. Add the whiskey, cloves, slice of lemon, and fill up with boiling water.

This is a favorite nightcap in Ireland. Very relaxing before going to bed. It is always taken to ward off a chill or an attack of influenza. Such pleasant medicine, too. *1 serving.*

EGG FLIP (1)

¾ cup milk	*1 jigger Irish whiskey*
1 egg yolk	*Grated nutmeg*
1 teaspoon sugar	

Scald the milk. Beat the egg yolk and sugar together. Add the whiskey and pour the scalding milk on top. Add the grated nutmeg and serve in a heated glass. This is an excellent pick-me-up and should be drunk at midmorning or midafternoon, when spirits are flagging. *1 serving.*

EGG FLIP (2)

Make as for EGG FLIP (1), but fold in the stiffly beaten white of an egg before serving. *1 serving.*

BLACK VELVET

This is a very snob drink and goes well with oysters. Also considered good for a hangover.

½ pint stout
¼ pint nonvintage champagne

Pour the stout into the champagne and serve in a tall glass. *1 serving.*

This is a good marriage—the champagne lightens the stout and the stout fortifies the champagne.

SLOE GIN

I mention sloe gin here because sloes are the fruit of the blackthorn, a very Irish shrub. When I was young, we always used poteen in place of gin. It was far cheaper and much stronger.

2 pints freshly picked sloes
1¾ cups lump sugar
1 quart gin

Prick the sloes with a fork. Crush about 12 of the sloes so that the kernels are broken. Put the sloes in bottles with the sugar and gin. Cork very tightly. Shake once a week for 6 months. Strain and rebottle.

This is the most beautiful ruby color you ever saw, and makes a delicious after-dinner liqueur.

Use the strained sloes to enliven an ice cream.

P.S. If you can't get sloes, try damson plums.

BLACK-CURRANT SYRUP

3 pounds black currants   Sugar
1¼ cups water   1 egg white

Remove the stalks from the berries. Crush the berries lightly
to release the juice, add the water. Put in a slow oven until
juice runs freely. Strain off the juice through muslin and measure
juice. To each cup of juice allow a half cup of sugar. Warm the
sugar in the oven. Put the juice in the pan with the beaten egg
white, and bring to the boil, whisking from time to time. Remove all scum and add the warmed sugar. When the sugar has
dissolved completely, bottle the syrup. If you want to keep the
syrup some time, add a teaspoon of Irish whiskey before cork-
ing. Store in refrigerator.

This syrup is excellent for children. A tablespoonful added
to a glass of hot water is very soothing for a sore throat. Full of
vitamins, too. *Yields about 1½ cups.*

HOMEMADE LEMONADE

3 lemons   3 cups boiling water
2 cups sugar
1 tablespoon tartaric or
   citric acid

Squeeze the juice from the lemons. Put the juice and skins into
a large jug with the sugar, acid, and boiling water. Stir to dissolve
sugar. Cover the jug with a plate and leave to get cold. Discard
lemon skins and bottle liquid. *Yields about 1 quart.*

To serve, put 2 tablespoons of the syrup in a glass. Fill up
with ice and soda water.
Nice for children.

GIN AND LEMON

1 jigger gin
½ tablespoon homemade lemonade
Ice

Mix all together and serve as a cocktail.   *1 serving.*

Nice for adults.

Index

Almond shortbread, 141
Appetizers: chicken livers, cold, 3
  crab cocktail, 5
  kippers, 6
  liver pâté, 2–3
  marinated kippers, 6
  pickled herrings, 5–6
  prawn cocktail, 4–5
  red caviar, 3–4
Apple fluff, 147
Applesauce, 85
Apple tart, 146
Artichoke soup, 13

Bacon: and egg tart, 96
  boiled, and cabbage, 67
  rinds, crushed, 110
Baked: custard, 149
  toffee, 149
Barmbrack, 134–35
Beef: corned, and cabbage, 50–51
  gravy, 48
  kidney soup, 17
  roast, 47–48
  spiced, Irish, 51–52
  steak and kidney stew, 50
  steak and onions, 48–49
  tea, Irish, 53–54
  tongue, pressed, 52–53
  top rib, 48
Beverages, 153–59
  black-currant syrup, 158
  black velvet, 157
  buttermilk, homemade, 120–21
  coffee, Irish, 155
  egg flip, 156
  gin and lemon, 159
  Irish coffee, 155
  Irish whiskey punch, 156
  lemonade, homemade, 158
  poteen, 154
  sloe gin, 157
  stout, 154
Black and white puddings, 72
Black-currant syrup, 158
Black velvet, 157
Boned chicken, 78–80
Boxty, 129
Brains, lamb, 59
Brandy butter, 150–51
Brawn, 72–73
Bread, 119–31
  baking utensils, 123
  boxty, 129
  brown, home-baked, 124–26
  griddle, 126
  Irish soda, 124
    ingredients, 122–23

  oatcakes: modern, 130
    old-fashioned, 129–30
  pancakes, 132
  porridge, 132–33
  potato cakes, 128
  sauce, 78
  scones: brown tea, 131
    tea, 131
  sour milk for Irish soda bread, 122
  treacle, 127
  yellow meal, 127
  See also Scones
Broth, mutton, 15
Brown bread, home-baked, 124–26
Brussels sprouts, 109
Butter: brandy, 150–51
  homemade, 120–21
  spongecake, 136
Buttermilk, homemade, 120–21

Cabbage, 67, 104–7
  creamed, 106–7
  salad, 107
  spring green, 105–6
  white, boiled, 106
Cakes, 134–41
  almond shortbread, 141
  apple tart, 146
  barmbrack, 134–35
  butter spongecake, 136
  cherry, 137
  Christmas, 139–40
  Dublin, 138
  fruitcake: barmbrack, 134–35
    Christmas, 139–40
    Dublin, 138
  Irish whiskey, 138–39
  meringues, simple, 141
  oatcakes, 129–30
  scones: tea, 131
    brown, 131
  seedcake, 136–37
  shortbread, almond, 141
  spongecake, 135
    butter, 136
  sponge lozenges, 136
  tea scones, 131
    brown, 131
  trifle, visitors', 145
Carrageen peppermint cream, 144
Carrots, 111–12
  baby, 111–12
  buttered, 111
Cauliflower, 110
Caviar, red, 3–4
Celery: sauce, 83
  soup, 12–13
Cereal. See Porridge

Champ, 102–3
Cheese sauce, 97
Cherry cake, 137
Chicken, 75–82
  and ham soup, 16–17
  boiled, 78
  boned, 78–80
  -bone stock, 10
  liver pâté, 2–3
  livers, cold, 3
  steamed breast of, 80–81
  stuffed roast, 77–78
  Tinkers', 81–82
Chocolate sauce, 144
Christmas: cake, 139–40
  goose, 85–86
  pudding. See Plum pudding
Clear soup, 18–19
Cod, 27–28
  roe, 29–30
  salt, creamed, 29
Coffee: custard, 149
  Irish, 155
  pudding, Irish, 143–44
Colcannon, 103–4
Consommé. See Clear soup
Corned beef and cabbage, 50–51
Crab, 39–41
  boiled, 39–40
  cocktail, 5
  creamed, 40
  in cheese sauce, 40–41
Creamed: cabbage, 106–7
  crab, 40
  salt cod, 29
  smoked haddock, 28–29
Crubeens (pig's feet), 73–74
Cucumber salad, 118
Custard, 145
  baked, 149
  baked toffee, 149
  coffee, 149

Desserts. See Cakes, Scones, Pies, and
    Puddings
Drinks. See Beverages
Drisheens, 72
Dublin Bay prawns. See Prawns
Dublin cake, 138
Dublin coddle, 71
Duck, 86–87. See also Wild duck

Egg(s), 93–99
  bacon and egg tart, 96
  flip, 156
  hot-buttered, 94–95
  mimosa, 98
  poached, and ham, 96–97
  preserved, with lard, 95
  roasted, 98
  soufflés, 99
  Wicklow pancake, 97

Fish and shellfish, 22–45
  cod, 27–28
    roe, 29–30
    salt, creamed, 29
  crab, 39–41

  boiled, 39–40
  cocktail, 5
  creamed, 40
  in cheese sauce, 40–41
haddock, 27–28
  smoked, creamed, 28–29
  smoked, soup, 21
  stuffed fillets of, 28
hake, 27–28
herring, 33
  broiled, 34
  fried, 33
  pickled, 5–6
  roes, 34
  See Kippers
kippers, 6
  marinated, 6
lobster, 36–38
  broiled, 37–38
  cold boiled, 37
  in a crust, 38
  roast, 38
mackerel, 34–35
  broiled, 35
  cold, 35
  in cider, 35
mussel(s), 43–45
  stew, 43–44
  with rice, 45
oysters, 45
prawn(s), 41
  cocktail, 4–5
  cocktail sauce, 5
  Dublin Bay, 41
  with mayonnaise, 41
salmon, 23–27
  cold, 25–26
  poached, 25
  smoked, fisherman's, 27
  steaks, broiled, 26
  steamed, 26
  whole, 24
  sauce: parsley butter. See Salmon steaks,
    broiled
scallops, 41–43
  in mushroom sauce, 42
  with cheese sauce, 42–43
shellfish soup, 20–21
smoked fish soup, 21
sole, broiled black, 31–32
trout, cured, 30–31
turtle soup, 19–20
whiting, 32
  fillets, 32–33
Fruit: apple(s):
  fluff, 147
  sauce, 85
  tart, 146
  black-currant syrup, 158
  flan. See Strawberry flan
  lemonade, homemade, 158
  lemon pudding, 148
  plum: pudding, 150–51
  strawberry: flan, 147–48
  tart. See Apple tart
Fruitcake: barmbrack, 134–35
  Christmas, 139–40
  Dublin, 138

Game, 87–92
Garlic, 117
Gin and lemon, 159
Goose, 84–86
  Christmas, 85–86
  Michaelmas, 84–85
Gravy, 48
  lamb, 55
  roast beef, 48
Griddle bread, 126
Grouse, 88–89
  roast, 88–89
  stewed, 89

Haddock, 27–28
  smoked, creamed, 28–29
  smoked, soup, 21
  stuffed fillets of, 28
Hake, 27–28
Ham, 68–70
  and poached egg, 96–97
  baked, Irish, 69–70
  boiled, Irish, 68–69
  See also Bacon
Herring, 33
  broiled, 34
  fried, 33
  pickled, 5–6
  roes, 34
  See also Kippers
Hot-buttered eggs, 94–95

Irish: beef tea, 53–54
  coffee, 155
  coffee pudding, 143–44
  peas, 114
  potato soup, 9–10
  sausages, 70–72
  soda bread, 124
    ingredients, 122–23
  spiced beef, 51–52
  stew, 60–62
  whiskey cake, 138–39
  whiskey punch, 156

Kidney(s): lamb, in their jackets, 58
  pork, and skirts, 66
  soup, 17
Kippers, 6
  marinated, 6

Lamb, 54–63
  boiled leg of, and parsley sauce, 56–57
  brains, 59
  heads, 59
  Irish stew, 60–62
  kidneys in their jackets, 58
  liver, 58
  roast leg of, 54–55
    in a crust, 55
  roast shoulder of, 57
  stew, 57
  sweetbreads, 58–59
  tongues and cheeks, 60
  tripe and onions, 62–63
Leek soup, 13
Lemonade, homemade, 158
Lemon pudding, 148

Liver: lamb, 58
  pâté, 2–3
Lobster, 36–38
  broiled, 37–38
  cold boiled, 37
  in a crust, 38
  roast, 38

Mackerel, 34–35
  broiled, 35
  cold, 35
  in cider, 35
Marinated kippers, 6
Masking sauce, 80
Meals, 120. See also Tea
Meats, 46–74
  bacon: and egg tart, 96
    boiled, and cabbage, 67
    rinds, crushed, 110
  beef: corned, and cabbage, 50–51
    gravy, 48
    kidney soup, 17
    roast, 47–48
    spiced, Irish, 51–52
    steak and kidney stew, 50
    steak and onions, 48–49
    tea, Irish, 53–54
    tongue, pressed, 52–53
    top rib, 48
  brains, lamb, 59
  clear soup, 18–19
  corned beef and cabbage, 50–51
  ham, 68–70
    and poached egg, 96–97
    baked, Irish, 69–70
    boiled, Irish, 68–69
    See also Bacon
  kidney(s): lamb, in their jackets, 58
    pork, and skirts, 66
    soup, 17
  lamb, 54–63
    boiled leg of, and parsley sauce, 56–57
    brains, 59
    heads, 59
    Irish stew, 60–62
    kidneys in their jackets, 58
    liver, 58
    roast leg of, 54–55
      in a crust, 55
    roast shoulder of, 57
    stew, 57
    sweetbreads, 58–59
    tongues and cheeks, 60
    tripe and onions, 62–63
  mutton, broth, 15
  pork, 63–74
    and apple stew, 65
    bacon: and egg tart, 96
      boiled, and cabbage, 67
      rinds, crushed, 110
    black and white puddings, 72
    brawn, 72–73
    ham, 68–70
      and poached egg, 96–97
      baked, Irish, 69–70
      boiled, Irish, 68–69
    liver pâté, 2–3
    pig's feet, boiled, 73–74

roast, 63–64
sausages, 70–72
drisheens, 72
Dublin coddle, 71
fried, 70–71
skirts and bodices, 66
skirts and kidneys, 66
steak, stuffed, 64–65
sausages, 70–72
drisheens, 72
Dublin coddle, 71
fried, 70–71
steak: and kidney stew, 50
and onions, 48–49
sweetbreads, lamb, 58–59
tongue: beef, pressed, 52–53
lamb, 60
tripe and onions, 62–63
Menus, xxiii–xxvi
Meringues, simple, 141
Michaelmas goose, 84–85
Milk, souring, for Irish soda bread, 122
Mimosa eggs, 98
Mincemeat, 151
Mince pies, 151–52
Molasses. See Treacle bread
Mushrooms, 115
in butter, 115–16
Mussel(s), 43–45
stew, 43–44
with rice, 45
Mutton broth, 15

Nettle tonic, 14–15

Oatcakes: modern, 130
old-fashioned, 129–30
Onion(s), 107–9
baked, 108–9
boiled, 108
soup, 11–12
pale, 11
Oysters, 45

Pancakes, 132
boxty, 129
oatcakes, 129–30
potato cakes, 128
Wicklow, 97
Parsley, 116
butter. See Salmon steaks, broiled
fried, 117
sauce, 17, 56
Parsnips, 112
toasted, 112
Pastry: piecrust, 152
shell, 147–48
short-crust, 96
Pâté, liver, 2–3
Pea(s), 113–14
frozen, 114
Irish, 114
soup, 14
Pheasant, 90
Pickled herrings, 5–6
Piecrust, 152

Pies: apple tart, 146
mince, 151–52
strawberry flan, 147–48
Pig's feet, boiled, 73–74
Plum pudding, 150–51
Poached egg and ham, 96–97
Poached salmon, 25
Pork, 63–74
and apple stew, 65
bacon: and egg tart, 96
boiled, and cabbage, 67
rinds, crushed, 110
black and white puddings, 72
brawn, 72–73
ham, 68–73
ham, 68–70
and poached egg, 96–97
baked, Irish, 69–70
boiled, Irish, 68–69
liver pâté, 2–3
pig's feet, boiled, 73–74
roast, 63–64
sausages, 70–72
skirts and bodices, 66
skirts and kidneys, 66
steak, stuffed, 64–65
Porridge, 132–33
Potato(es): baked jacket, 102
boxty, 129
cakes, 128
champ, 102–3
colcannon, 103–4
flounces, 104
new, boiled, 101
roast, 102
soup, Irish, 9–10
stuffing, 84–85
Poteen, 154
Poultry and game, 75–91
chicken, 75–82
and ham soup, 16–17
boiled, 78
boned, 78–80
-bone stock, 10
liver pâté, 2–3
livers, cold, 3
steamed breast of, 80–81
stuffed roast, 77–78
tinkers', 81–82
duck, 86–87
game, 87–92
goose, 84–86
Christmas, 85–86
Michaelmas, 84–85
grouse, 88–89
roast, 88–89
stewed, 89
pheasant, 90
rabbit, 91
stew, 91–92
snipe, 90
stuffings: for roast chicken, 77
potato, 84–85
turkey, 82–84
boiled, and celery sauce, 82–83
Uncle George's, 83–84
venison, 90–91

wild duck, roast, 87
woodcock, 90
Prawn(s), 41
  cocktail, 4–5
  cocktail sauce, 5
  Dublin Bay, 41
  with mayonnaise, 41
Preserved eggs, 95
Puddings, 142–51
  apple fluff, 147
  Carrageen peppermint cream, 144
  custard, 145
    baked, 149
    baked toffee, 149
    coffee, 149
  Irish coffee pudding, 143–44
  lemon, 148
  plum, 150–51
  trifle, visitors', 145

Rabbit, 91
  stew, 91–92
Red caviar, 3–4
Roast beef, 47–48
Roasted eggs, 98

Salads: cabbage, 107
  cucumber, 118
Salmon, 23–27
  cold, 25–26
  poached, 25
  smoked, fisherman's, 27
  steaks, broiled, 26
  steamed, 26
  whole, 24
Sauces: brandy butter, 150–51
  bread, 78
  celery, 83
  cheese, 97
  chocolate, 144
  masking, 80
  parsley, 17, 56
  parsley butter. See Salmon steaks, broiled
  prawn cocktail, 5
  thickening, 44
Sausages, Irish, 70–72
Scallops, 41–43
  in mushroom sauce, 42
  with cheese sauce, 42–43
Scones, 131
Seedcake, 136–37
Shellfish soup, 20–21
Shortbread, almond, 141
Skirts and bodices, 66
Skirts and kidneys, 66
Sloe gin, 157
Smoked fish soup, 21
Smoked haddock, creamed, 28–29
Smoked salmon, fisherman's, 27
Snipe, 90
Sole, broiled black, 31–32
Soufflés, 99
Soups, 7–21
  artichoke, 13
  celery, 12–13
  chicken and ham, 16–17
  chicken-bone stock, 10
  clear, 18–19

consommé. See Clear soup
  Irish potato, 9–10
  kidney, 17
  leek, 13
  mutton broth, 15
  nettle tonic, 14–15
  onion, 11–12
    pale, 11
  pea, 14
  shellfish, 20–21
  smoked fish, 21
  stock, chicken-bone, 10
  turtle, 19–20
  See also Broth and Consommé
Spiced beef, Irish, 51–52
Spongecake, 135
  butter, 136
Sponge lozenges, 136
Spring green cabbage, 105–6
Steak: and kidney stew, 50
  and onions, 48–49
Steamed salmon, 26
Stew: Irish, 60–62
  lamb, 57
  mussel, 43–44
  pork and apple, 65
  rabbit, 91–92
  steak and kidney, 50
Stock, soup, 10
Stout, 154
Strawberry flan, 147–48
Stuffed fillets of haddock, 28
Stuffing: for roast chicken, 77
  for pork steak, 64
  potato, 84–85
Sweetbreads, lamb, 58–59

Tarts: apple, 146
  bacon and egg, 96
Tea: pancakes, 132
  scones, 131
  six-o'clock, 120
Thickening sauce, 44
Tinkers' chicken, 81–82
Tongue: beef, pressed, 52–53
  lamb, 60
Treacle bread, 127
Trifle, visitors', 145
Tripe and onions, 62–63
Trout, cured, 30–31
Turkey, 82–84
  boiled, and celery sauce, 82–83
  Uncle George's, 83–84
Turnips, 112, 113
  mashed, 113
Turtle soup, 19–20

Vegetables, 110–18
  artichoke soup, 13
  brussels sprouts, 109
  cabbage, 67, 104–7
    creamed, 106–7
    salad, 107
    spring green, 105–6
    white, boiled, 106
  carrots, 111–12
    baby, 111–12
    buttered, 111

cauliflower, 110
celery: sauce, 83
    soup, 12–13
champ, 102–3
colcannon, 103–4
cucumber, salad, 118
garlic, 117
leek soup, 13
mushrooms, 115
    in butter, 115–16
nettles, tonic, 14–15
onions, 107–9
    baked, 108–9
    boiled, 108
    soup, 11–12
parsley, 116
    butter. *See* Salmon steaks, broiled
    fried, 117
    sauce, 17, 56
parsnips, 112
peas, 113–14
    soup, 14

potato(es): baked jacket, 102
    boxty, 129
    cakes, 128
    champ, 102–3
    colcannon, 103–4
    flounces, 104
    new, boiled, 101
    roast, 102
    soup, Irish, 9–10
    stuffing, 84–85
turnips, 112, 113
Venison, 90–91

White cabbage. *See under* Cabbage
Whiting, 32
    fillets, 32–33
Wicklow pancake, 97
Wild duck, roast, 87
Woodcock, 90

Yellow meal bread, 127